D0734283

GRACE LIVINGSTON HILL

FOR EACH NEW DAY

365 Daily Devotions
from America's Most Beloved
Inspirational Author

A BARBOUR BOOK

Published by   Barbour and Company, Inc.
              P.O. Box 719
              Uhrichsville, OH 44683

Typesetting by Typetronix, Inc., Cape Coral, Florida
Printed in the United States of America

JANUARY

The Lord knows the end from the beginning, and nothing is surer than that He uses His children to carry out His plans.

"He knoweth thy walking through this great wilderness."
DEUTERONOMY 2:7

This is my verse when I am discouraged: "Wait on the Lord; be of good courage and he shall strengthen thine heart: wait, I say, on the Lord."

"No word He hath spoken,
Was ever yet broken."

"Pity's sake! if you weren't going to be a better woman by ten thousand times when you get to heaven than you are here, why, heaven would be an out and out disappointment, that's all," said Priscilla Hunter.

"And as we have borne the image of the earthly, we shall also bear the image of the heavenly." 1 CORINTHIANS 15:49

Conscience, working all alone, is a very uncomfortable and disagreeable companion, and often accomplishes for the time being nothing beyond making his victim disagreeable.

"Their conscience also bearing witness, and their thoughts the meanwhile accusing or else excusing one another." ROMANS 2:15

You take a diamond and throw it down in the dirt and filth, and put your foot on it and grind it in, and leave it there, sinking and soiling, day after day, year after year, and when somebody comes along and picks it out, how much will it gleam for Him at first? Yet the diamond is there.

"Thou shalt be a crown of glory in the hand of the Lord, and a royal diadem in the hand of thy God." ISAIAH 62:3

"Peace with God!" It expresses *so* much! Peace is greater than joy, or comfort, or rest.

"And let the peace of God rule in your hearts, to the which also you are called in one body." COLOSSIANS 3:15

Mine is the *doing* when He says the word, but His is the bringing to pass. And that, you see, is the end of all worrying and planning and doubt. There is no rest nor comfort outside of that conclusion.

"Then he said unto the man, Stretch forth thine hand. And he stretched it forth, and it was restored whole, like as the other."
MATTHEW 12:13

A sweet-faced cooing baby, arrayed in fine white-broidered garments, with bright eyes and dimpled chin, and mouth that breaks into radiant smiles whenever one looks that way, is an exquisite bit of enjoyment for anybody.

"And when she saw that he was a goodly child she hid him three months."
EXODUS 2:2

What a fearful world it would be if things just *happened*, with nobody to manage or control!

"For the eyes of the Lord run to and fro throughout the whole earth, to show himself strong in the behalf of them whose heart is perfect toward him."
2 CHRONICLES 16:19

We grieve sometimes that we cannot know people's hearts, and foresee what would please, and what would irritate. Hearts calm down wonderfully sometimes; what need then to know of their depths while at boiling point? But what sights must the all-seeing God look down upon! Sights in tenderness shut away from the gaze of His weak children.

"For He knoweth the secrets of the heart."   PSALM 44:21

JANUARY 11TH

"Diligent in business, serving the Lord." There is no period dividing these. I long ago discovered that I could make a bed and sweep a room for His sake, as surely as I could speak a word for Him.

"Faith is the golden thread on which we string for offering,
Our feeble deeds of poor self-sacrifice;
Unworthy gifts, yet in His grace, the King
Accounts them pearls of price."

JANUARY 12TH

I know people who suppose it would be almost irreverent to take their domestic bewilderments to Christ. I cannot think what kind of a friend they imagine Him to be, if they are afraid to go to Him with everything.

"Commit thy way unto the Lord; trust also in him; and he shall bring it to pass."   PSALM 37:5

JANUARY 13TH

Although the Lord is gracious and forbearing, and kindly gives me the work to do here and there for Him, He can, when He chooses, get along entirely without any help.

"For of him, and through him, and to him, are all things: to whom be glory forever."   ROMANS 11:36

JANUARY 14TH

You may often speak words which spring up, and bear fruit that reaches up to God; though you do not know it, and *will* not, until in heaven you take your crown, and question why there are so many stars.

"Be thou faithful unto death, and I will give thee a crown of life."
                                                                    REVELATION 2:10

JANUARY 15TH

The heart must understand that whatever the Lord directs it *intends* to do, or there is no opening of the door for Him.

"All that the Lord hath said we will do, and be obedient."
                                                                    EXODUS 24:7

JANUARY 16TH

To God, nothing that an immortal soul can say, appears trivial, because he sees the waves of influence which are stirred years ahead by the quiet words.

> *"Words are things of little cost,*
> *Quickly spoken, quickly lost;*
> *We forget them, but they stand*
> *Witnesses at God's right hand;*
> *And their testimony bear*
> *For us, or against us there."*

There is no place on the road so dark but that the Bible can light you through, if you try it. When you don't understand it, there is always Jesus to go to, you know.

"Thy word is a lamp unto my feet, and a light unto my path."
PSALM 119:105

God's son! To go to *Him*, saying, "Father, what shall I do about this?" and, "What would you advise as to that?"

"I will be his God, and he shall be my son."   REVELATION 21:7

God never promised to compromise with his own, never promised to hear a prayer which began with an "If." Entire consecration means all the "ifs" thrown down at the feet of the Lord for Him to control as He will.

"Nevertheless, not as I will, but as thou wilt."   MATTHEW 26:39

Is it so strange a thing that the Lord can keep his *own?*

"He will not suffer thy foot to be moved: He that keepeth thee will not slumber.

Behold, He that keepeth Israel shall neither slumber nor sleep.
The Lord is thy keeper: the Lord is thy shade upon thy right hand."

PSALM 121:3

It is wonderful, after all, how rarely in this wicked world we meet with other than respect in answer to a frank avowal of our determination to be on the Lord's side.

"Wherefore Thou art great, O, Lord God: for there is none like Thee, neither is there any God beside Thee, according to all that we have heard with our ears."

2 SAMUEL 7:22

Individual effort is so necessary that I have thought perhaps the Holy Spirit turns our thoughts most directly toward one person at a time, so that we may concentrate our efforts.

"While Peter thought on the vision, the Spirit said unto him, Behold, three men seek thee.
Arise therefore, and get thee down, and go with them, doubting nothing: for I have sent them."

ACTS 10:19

I don't know how a thoughtful man can ever reject the idea of an overruling Providence.

"The fool hath said in his heart, There is no God."

PSALM 53:1

Shall you and I ever stand beside a new-made grave, receiving one whom we have known ever so slightly, and have to settle with our conscience and our Saviour, because we have not invited that one to come to Jesus?

"And the Lord said unto Cain, Where is Abel thy brother? And he said, I know not: am I my brother's keeper?" GENESIS 4:9

Never mind whether you are *now* one of His children or not; claim the place of a child because you need to be, and wish to be, and *mean* to be one from this moment.

"Beloved, now are we the sons of God." 1 JOHN 15:6

"She came finally to understand that the point was not, Was I a Christian last year, or last week, or even yesterday? but, Do I mean to be one to-day — now?"

"If a man abide not in Me, he is cast forth as a branch, and is withered; and men gather them, and cast them into the fire, and they are burned.' JOHN 15:6

The flush had died away from Ruth's face; she was growing very pale. This was a rapid descent from the mount whereon she had been standing: only a moment before, she had felt as though earth and its commonplaces could not touch her again; because she had been permitted for a moment to stand face to face with Jesus Christ. Yet here was the keen, cruel world at her very elbow!

"In the world ye shall have tribulation: but be of good comfort: I have overcome the world."   JOHN 16:33

I don't know whether it will work or not; and what is more, I never shall know until I try. There has many a thing been accomplished in this world that never would have been, had people settled it in their minds that it couldn't be done before they had made vigorous efforts to *do* it.

"I can do all things through Christ which strengtheneth me."   PHILIPPIANS 4:13

Isn't it pleasant to think that in all those little things He is watching over you, and that you make Him glad when you do them well?

"He that is faithful in that which is least is faithful also in much: and he that is unjust in the least is unjust also in much."   LUKE 16:10

"Cleanse thou me from secret faults," prayed the inspired writer. May he not have meant those faults so secret that it takes the voice of God to reveal them to our hearts?

"For the Lord seeth not as man seeth; for man looketh on the outward appearance, but the Lord looketh on the heart." 1 SAMUEL 16:7

JANUARY 31ST

I can think of a good many things which we call right enough, that, measured by Paul's test, would have to be given up.

"But take heed lest by any means this liberty of yours become a stumbling block to them that are weak." 1 CORINTHIANS 8:9

FEBRUARY

"Who forgiveth all thine iniquities."

What a salvation! Able to forgive transgression, to cover sin, to remember it no more.

> *"Bearing shame and scoffing rude,*
> *In my place condemned He stood;*
> *Sealed my pardon with His blood:*
> *Hallelujah, what a Saviour!"*

You can find plenty of work if you look for it; only don't look too far, because it is the little bits of things, which come right in your way, that Jesus wants you to do.

"Well done, thou good and faithful servant; thou hast been faithful over a few things, I will make thee ruler over many things: enter thou into the joy of thy Lord."　　　　　MATTHEW 25:21

You don't know what a relief it is to go right to the Lord with your worries.

"Casting all your care upon him; for he careth for you."

1 PETER 5:7

FEBRUARY 4TH

There will be no such thing as that hateful word "disappointment" up in heaven, bless the Lord; haven't I His own word for it? Didn't He say we should be satisfied? I wonder what it feels like to be *satisfied*!

"I shall be satisfied when I awake with thy likeness."

PSALM 17:15

FEBRUARY 5TH

It did not say: "My grace is sufficient for the great and trying experiences of this life, but for the little every day annoyances and trials which tempt you — you must look out for yourself." It was just an unlimited promise.

"God is faithful, who will not suffer you to be tempted above that ye are able; but will with the temptation also make a way to escape, that ye may be able to bear it." 1 CORINTHIANS 10:13

FEBRUARY 6TH

I take it that God permits all faithful service to be for His glory.

"That we should be to the praise of his glory, who first trusted in Christ." EPHESIANS 1:12

Of course some change must come; nothing ever stayed for any length of time, just as it was; but what would the change be? It came in an unexpected manner, perhaps that is the common way with changes.

"Watch ye, therefore; for ye know not when the master of the house cometh — Lest coming suddenly, he find you sleeping."
MARK 13:35

Every woman owns a little piece of the world; I do, so does everybody, why *can't* each one look out for her own little corner?

"Every one over against his house."   NEHEMIAH 3:28

It is His own voice speaking. Go to Him for help, and as sure as the sun shines above these clouds you will get just what you need.

"So the Lord shall make bright clouds."   ZECHARIAH 10:1

"Then said Jesus, If ye *continue* in my words, then are ye my disciples indeed." Just think how far that reaches! All through the words of Jesus. So many of them, so many things to do, and so many *not* to do; and then not only to begin to follow them, but to *continue;* day after day getting a little farther, and knowing a little more.

"Till we all come in the unity of the faith, and of the knowledge of the Son of God, unto a perfect man, unto the measure of the stature of the fullness of Christ."   EPHESIANS 4:13

FEBRUARY 11TH

In point of fact, it is not often that He calls upon people to make the sacrifice which Satan tries to push into their minds as a fearful one; but whether He does or not is not then the question. Having allowed a "what if" to come into your heart, you must get rid of it by the determination to do *whatever* He says, or you really cannot belong to Him, however much you may wish it.

"Whatsoever He saith unto you, do it."   JOHN 2:5

FEBRUARY 12TH

To live so that when people spoke of me at all, the most marked thing they could say about me would be, not how I dressed, or appeared, or talked, but how strong my faith in the Lord Jesus was, and how it colored all my words and acts. Wouldn't that be a grand ambition?

"And they took knowledge of them, that they had been with Jesus."
ACTS 4:13

FEBRUARY 13TH

Suppose Christ should forgive only those who had treated him well; would you be forgiven to-day?

"But if ye forgive not men their trespasses, neither will your Father forgive your trespasses." MATTHEW 6:15

Why can't *Christian* people at least, see that they have no right to consult their own inclinations? that the object is to save souls, and bodies, and that in every conceivable place, and at every possible time, when an opportunity is offered, it is their duty to put themselves where they will be sure to be counted on the right side?

"She hath done what she could." MARK 14:8

Are you quite happy as a Christian? Do you find your love growing stronger and your hopes brighter from day to day?

"But grow in grace, and in the knowledge of our Lord and Saviour Jesus Christ." 2 PETER 3:18

"He could not do many mighty works there because of their unbelief." I think that is what is the matter with the world to-day. I wonder if He would not be pleased with one who could throw herself at His feet with a childlike abandon of faith, and expect wonders, yes, and impossibilities, just as a child feels that *anything* can be done by father?

"If our faith were but more simple,
We should take Him at His word,
And our lives would be all sunshine
In the sweetness of our Lord."

My dear friend, you have really no right to set a different time from the one that your Master has set. Don't you know that His time is always *now?*

"Behold, now is the accepted time; behold, now is the day of salvation."
2 CORINTHIANS 6:2

Sometimes the people whom we meet but once, with whom we really have very little to do, are given a word to say, or an act to perform, that shall influence all our future lives.

"What manner of persons ought ye to be in all holy conversation and godliness?"
2 PETER 3:11

If somebody had only bent down to him, and whispered a few words, just to set his poor wandering feet into the narrow way, how blessed it would have been! but nobody did.

Ah, never mind! God knew, and took care of him.

"And let him that heareth say, Come."   REVELATION 22:17

Perchance that sleeping Christian might have been startled and aroused, could she have realized that days like those would never come back to her; that being misspent they had passed away.

"Awake thou that sleepest, and arise from the dead, and Christ shall give thee light."   EPHESIANS 5:14

Did you never wonder that some portion some little sentence from the Bible, should so forcibly impress your mind, and so cling to you? Perhaps you tried to drive it away, so much did it trouble you, but still it hovered around, and seemed to keep repeating itself over and over to your heart. Be not deceived. This was Jesus of Nazareth passing by and waiting for you to say, "Jesus, thou Son of David, have mercy on me."

"For the word of God is quick, and powerful, and sharper than any two-edged sword."   HEBREWS 4:12

One mischief with Christians is, that when they sit down to think of these matters, they are not personal. I am apt to ask whether *people* act as though they thought religion the most important matter in life, instead of asking whether I have this day lived as though I thought religion the most important matter with which I had to do.

"Is it well with thee?"   2 KINGS 4:26

Clearly if she wanted the sun, it was her part to open blinds and draw back curtains; clearly if she wanted mental light, it was her part to use the means that God had placed at her disposal.

"Work out your own salvation with fear and trembling. For it is God which worketh in you both to will and to do of his good pleasure."
PHILIPPIANS 2:12

We are all too willing to be conquered, not willing to reach after and obtain the settled and ever-growing joys of the Christian.

"O that thou hadst hearkened to my commandments! then had thy peace been as a river, and thy righteousness as the waves of the sea."
ISAIAH 48:18

Now what you need to remember, is, that the Lord is your father, whether you choose to own Him or not; and He has a right to your love, and your help.

"Do ye thus requite the Lord, O foolish people and unwise? is not he thy father that hath bought thee? hath he not made thee and established thee?"
DEUTERONOMY 32:6

Conversion is *change of heart*, and a heart given up to the reign of Christ, the supreme desire being to please Him, will, at the outset, be a very different heart from the one that was given up to the reign of self.

"That they which live should not henceforth live unto themselves, but unto him which died for them, and rose again."

2 Corinthians 5:15

FEBRUARY 27TH

If my Christian life were so marked a force that all who came in contact with me felt its influence, it would be natural to speak of it, when my friends chanced to mention my name.

"I heard of your faith in the Lord Jesus." Ephesians 1:15

FEBRUARY 28TH

There's a thing to remember; that you don't belong to yourself at all; and are bound to do the best you can with your time, and strength, and everything.

"What, know ye not that your body is the temple of the Holy Ghost which is in you, which ye have of God, and ye are not your own?"

1 Corinthians 6:19

FEBRUARY 29TH

He has infinite power, and infinite wisdom, and infinite forgiveness. There is nothing that He cannot forgive, and nothing that He cannot help you to do, if it is right that you should do it. I speak with authority, for I have tried Him; yes, with better authority than that — for He has said it.

"He shall deliver thee in six troubles: yea, in seven there shall no evil touch thee."   JOB 5:19

MARCH

Did you ever tell Him all about it? Of course He knows, yet His direction is that for our own sakes we tell Him the story.

"Oh, leave it all with Jesus,
Drooping soul!
Tell not half thy story,
But the whole.
Worlds on worlds are hanging
On His hand,
Life and death are waiting
His command;
Yet His tender bosom
Makes thee room — Oh, come home!"

Don't you think that some of our trouble is in being content with simply reading, not studying the Bible?

"Search the scriptures; for in them ye think ye have eternal life: and they are they which testify of me." **JOHN 5:39**

"God will not call me to account for *your* undone work, only my own."

"For the work of a man shall he render unto him, and cause every man to find according to his ways." JOB 34:11

We have need of missionaries right here at home; we must evangelize the church of Christ, and get it to take hold of its privileges!

"He that hath an ear let him hear what the Spirit saith unto the churches; To him that overcometh will I give to eat of the hidden manna, and will give him a white stone, and in the stone a new name written, which no man knoweth save he that receiveth it." REVELATION 2:17

Is it possible that I have been one of those faithless disciples, rebuking, or at least ignoring, the presence of one of His little ones, while I reached out after fruit that I dared to think was of more importance!

"And whoso shall receive one such little child in my name, receiveth me." MATTHEW 18:5

It doesn't seem to me that it is money, or time, or strength, or talent, that is lacking, it is the consecrated heart. A heart that is given first to Christ, and secondly, to His work, whatever form it may take, or whatever may be the door that opens.

"And who then is willing to consecrate his service this day unto the Lord?"   1 Chronicles 29:5

MARCH 7TH

Isn't it strange that the followers of Christ will go on, year after year, bending a listening ear to Satan, while he rings the changes of that old, long-ago, vanished falsehood, "If thou be the Son of God?"

"Above all, taking the shield of faith, wherewith ye shall be able to quench all the fiery darts of the wicked."   Ephesians 6:16

MARCH 8TH

"To the saints and faithful brethren in Christ which are at Colosse." Suppose we had been living at Colosse in those days, could we have claimed that letter to the saints?

"Beloved of God, called to be saints."   Romans 1:7

MARCH 9TH

The man who seems to me the most worthy of contempt, is the one who has not sufficient moral courage to break a promise after he discovers that it ought never to have been made.

"Hearken unto me, ye that know righteousness, the people in whose heart is my law; fear ye not the reproach of men, neither be ye afraid of their revilings."
                                                            ISAIAH 51:7

MARCH 10TH

We haven't to do anything about it until to-morrow; perhaps to-morrow will have a light of its own for our direction.

"Take therefore no thought for the morrow; for the morrow shall take thought for the things of itself. Sufficient unto the day is the evil thereof."
                                                            MATTHEW 6:34

MARCH 11TH

We depend too much on tact and too little on God's spirit. "Open thy mouth and I will fill it," is a promise that applies to more places than a prayer meeting, I think.

"Now therefore go, and I will be with thy mouth, and teach thee what thou shalt say."
                                                            EXODUS 4:12

MARCH 12TH

"I do not wonder that, looking at me, you have grown into the habit of thinking that there is nothing in religion," she said. "You have looked at me, not at Jesus, and there has been no reflection of his beauty in me, as there should have been, and the result is not strange."

"But we all, with open face beholding as in a glass the glory of the Lord, are changed into the same image from glory to glory, even as by the spirit of the Lord." 2 CORINTHIANS 3:18

MARCH 13TH

I know I love the Lord, and I know that he will not destroy me, for I have in my heart the assurance of His promise.

"The Lord preserveth all them that love him: but all the wicked will he destroy." PSALM 145:20

MARCH 14TH

You will find that it needs precisely the same help to meet trifles that it does to conquer mountains of difficulty. The difference is in degree, not in kind.

"Surely he shall deliver thee from the snare of the fowler, and from the noisome pestilence." PSALM 91:3

MARCH 15TH

"Commit thy way unto the Lord." How much pleasanter it would have been to have committed it in the first place, before I wearied my heart with worrying over what I could not lift my finger to make different!

> *"O holy trust! O endless sense of rest!*
> *Like the beloved John*
> *To lay his head upon the Saviour's breast,*
> *And then to journey on."*

I believe a consecrated life will be honored by the Lord in whatever channel He gives it talents to develop.

"Say ye to the righteous that it shall be well with him."
ISAIAH 3:10

If people only *would* influence each other just as much as they could, and just as *high* as they could, what a wonderful thing this living would be!

"That ye may be blameless and harmless, the sons of God, without rebuke, in the midst of a crooked and perverse nation, among whom ye shine as lights in the world."
PHILIPPIANS 2:15

There are ten thousand little things no more important in themselves than brushing out troublesome flies, or shutting out glaring sunlight, or tidying a slovenly washstand, or cooling a burning forehead, which can be used as nets wherewith to catch poor, tired, homesick fish.

"And Jesus said unto them, Come ye after me, and I will make you to become fishers of men."
MARK 1:17

Dear friend, whatever you are, no matter what mistakes you have made, no matter how unfit you feel, you are dear to Christ at this moment: He loves you and waits for you.

"I have loved thee with an everlasting love: therefore with lovingkindness have I drawn thee." JEREMIAH 31:3

MARCH 20TH

Softly there came another voice. "What of all that?" it said; "suppose nobody cares for you, or helps you here. Jesus died, you know, and He is your friend."

"If God be for us who can be against us?" ROMANS 8:31

MARCH 21ST

I have an all-absorbing, a consuming ambition; it is to have the King put His hand on mine, and say, "Well done, good and faithful servant." I shall not be content without the commendation promised to those who faithfully serve; my ambition craves it.

"In the light of the king's countenance is life; and his favor is as a cloud of the latter rain." PROVERBS 16:15

MARCH 22ND

Of course you cannot help these bitter feelings; do you suppose He expects you to do so? If you could make your heart right yourself, where would be the need of His help?

"O my God, incline thine ear, and hear; . . . for we do not present our

supplications before thee for our righteousness, but for thy great mercies."

DANIEL 9:18

MARCH 23RD

It is grand to think that even the street-car driver can drive for the glory of God.

"And whatsoever ye do in word or deed, do all in the name of the Lord Jesus, giving thanks to God and the Father by him."

COLOSSIANS 3:17

MARCH 24TH

"Do with thy might whatsoever thy hand findeth to do," is our commission, you know, and in order to *find* things, we have to look for them.

"And what doth the Lord require of thee, but to do justly, and to love mercy, and to walk humbly with thy God?"

MICAH 6:8

MARCH 25TH

If I belong to Christ, I *belong*, don't I? There is no half-way service possible. Why do I not so look that others take knowledge of me that I have been with Jesus?

"Because that which may be known of God is manifest in them; for God hath showed it unto them."

ROMANS 1:19

Is it right for any servant of the King to mingle familiarly for an afternoon with others who either are, or should be, loyal subjects, and not make a definite impression for the King?

"Only let your conversation be as becometh the Gospel of Christ."
PHILIPPIANS 1:27

If one would be sympathetic with his kind, there is this thing always to remember: it is much easier to sit in a quiet room, surrounded with an atmosphere of peace, and talk about the petty trials of others, and the duty of bearing them cheerfully, than it is to belong to that other company who are at that moment in the heat of the conflict between duty and inclination.

"We then that are strong ought to bear the infirmities of them that are weak, and not to please ourselves."
ROMANS 15:1

Dear friend, I think you know where to look for help, no matter what your trial or burden; whether it be great or very small, He is equally ready to have it brought to Him and left there. Why don't you ask His help? You are one of His own.

"The Lord thy God in the midst of thee is mighty; he will save, he will rejoice over thee with joy; he will rest in his love, he will joy over thee with singing."
ZEPHANIAH 3:17

Hereafter when I feel particularly tried with a person, I shall know that I am myself at fault toward that person, and shall ask God for a special view of my own heart concerning it.

"Renew a right spirit within me."   PSALM 51:10

A great deal of money and a great deal of force, which might do wonders elsewhere, are wasted on dress.

"Whose adorning let it not be that outward adorning of plaiting the hair, and of wearing of gold, or of putting on of apparel."
1 PETER 3:3

The fact is, that to sit in a pleasant room, among one's friends, and discuss the inconsistencies of Christians, is one thing; and to go out into the world in the thick of the fight, and live consistently, is quite another.

"Be watchful, and strengthen the things which remain, that are ready to die: for I have not found thy works perfect before God."
REVELATION 3:2

APRIL

How many springtimes have you gone to your bed feeling that the season was late, and the trees were bare, and the fruits would all be backward, and Nature was dawdling along in a very wearisome fashion; and awakened in the morning to find that there had in the night been a gentle rain, and a movement of mysterious power among the buds and grasses, and that now in the morning sunshine, the world had burst into bloom? Yet, did you really suppose, after all, that the *work* was done in one night?

"For as the earth bringeth forth her bud, and the garden causeth the things that are sown in it to spring forth; so the Lord God will cause righteousness and praise to spring forth before all the nations."

ISAIAH 61:11

Since God has called us to honorable positions, even to be "co-laborers," shall we not rejoice in the honor?

"For we are laborers together with God."   1 CORINTHIANS 3:9

It is my joy that He has not separated any moment of my life from Him, saying, "Here is so much drudgery each day, from which I must be entirely separated; then, when that is done, you may serve me." Work so divided would be drudgery indeed.

"For in him we live, and move, and have our being."
ACTS 17:28

How many people have such marked and abiding faith in Christ Jesus, that when we talk of them we say, "I heard that Miss So and So had the most implicit faith in the power of Christ to keep her?" Now wouldn't that be a strange thing to say?

"We heard of your faith in Christ Jesus."   COLOSSIANS 1:4

A great sorrow is a wonderful educator.

"For it became him, for whom are all things, and by whom are all things, in bringing many sons unto glory, to make the captain of their salvation perfect through sufferings."   HEBREWS 2:10

It is, perhaps, to be questioned whether loneliness is, after all, demoralizing in its effects.

"Now no chastening for the present seemeth to be joyous, but grievous: nevertheless afterward it yieldeth the peaceable fruit of righteousness unto them which are exercised thereby." HEBREWS 12:11

What a thing it would be to be high in favor with God; to be so familiar at court that you could present a friend there, without a fear or doubt as to the result.

"Elias was a man subject to like passions as we are, and he prayed earnestly that it might not rain: and it rained not on the earth by the space of three years and six months.
And he prayed again, and the heaven gave rain, and the earth brought forth her fruit." JAMES 5:17

It is possible that you have not come in close contact with Christ's intimate friends. There are degrees in friendship, you know.

"Ye are my friends, if ye do whatsoever I command you." JOHN 15:14

"In my Father's house are many mansions; I go to prepare a place for you."
After all, that is the place for brightness. This is only a way station; never mind the discomforts, so that many are helped to the

right road and the home be reached at last, in peace.

"When the shore is won at last,
Who will count the billows past?"

Unpaid vows! — only think of it. Isn't it startling when we remember to whom they are due?

"When thou vowest a vow unto God, defer not to pay it; for he hath no pleasure in fools: pay that which thou hast vowed."
ECCLESIASTES 5:4

That very kettle which gives you Monday morning trouble can help you to a first victory: and it is a symbol of all the other things, small in themselves, but amounting to much, counted together, that can be made to serve you to-day.

"And hast borne, and hast patience, and for my name's sake hast laboured, and hast not fainted."
REVELATION 2:3

He made the plants and flowers — created their beauty for them, I mean, because they are soulless things — He left to us who are immortal, a great deal of the fashioning to do for ourselves.

"Finally, brethren, whatsoever things are true, whatsoever things are honest, whatsoever things are just, whatsoever things are pure, whatsoever things are lovely, whatsoever things are of good report; if there be any virtue, and if there be any praise, think on these things."
PHILIPPIANS 4:8

APRIL 13TH

What we need most to overcome is the idea that there is anything wicked in talking about religion in an everyday tone, as we talk about other topics of absorbing interest.

"Talk ye of all his wondrous works." 1 CHRONICLES 16:9

APRIL 14TH

If the Lord Jesus Christ can forgive him, I think we ought to be able to do so.

"And be ye kind one to another, tenderhearted, forgiving one another, even as God for Christ's sake hath forgiven you." PSALM 105:2

APRIL 15TH

Isn't it all different forms of the Master's work? The children of the home may have each a different task, but each is needed to make the home what it should be, and each worker needs the same spirit of love and unselfishness to enable him to do his part.

"For as we have many members in one body, and all members have not the same office:

So we, being many, are one body in Christ, and every one members one of another." ROMANS 12:5

A Christian home! It cannot simply mean a home where Christ is honored. It rather means a home where everything pertaining to it serves His cause. The very furniture, and the light and the brightness are made to do duty for Him, else they have no place there. What is there that I can do with all the beauties of my parlors?

"For none of us liveth to himself, and no man dieth to himself.
For whether we live, we live unto the Lord: and whether we die, we die unto the Lord: whether we live therefore, or die, we are the Lord's."
ROMANS 14:7

What an immense book the history of a human life would make! Probably no one will ever know how large a volume it would be, for no one will ever write it.

"And there are also many other things which Jesus did, the which, if they should be written every one, I suppose that even the world itself could not contain the books that should be written." JOHN 21:25

If we want to hear how living, growing Christians talk, we must frequent the places where we shall be likely to find them.

"Then they that feared the Lord spake often one to another: and the Lord hearkened, and heard it, and a book of remembrance was written before him for them that feared the Lord, and that thought upon his name."   MALACHI 3:16

The One who made such lovely plants and finished them so exquisitely, must be pleased to see us study enough of His works to make ourselves look pleasing to the eyes of others.

"He hath made everything beautiful in his time."
ECCLESIASTES 3:11

He made some mistakes; for he fancied, in his ignorance, that the struggle was over — that he had only to go forward joyfully over a pleasant road.

He found out his mistake; he discovered that Satan had not by any means given him up; that he must yet fight many hard, hard battles.

"Fight the good fight of faith, lay hold on eternal life, whereunto thou art also called, and hast professed a good profession before many witnesses."   1 TIMOTHY 6:12

I wonder when the world will learn that promises are solemn things, and that living is serious business, and that when we are young we are not called upon to decide questions which belong to mature judgments.

"Rejoice, O young man, in thy youth; and let thy heart cheer thee in the days of thy youth, and walk in the ways of thine heart, and in the sight of thine eyes: but know thou, for all these things God will bring thee into judgment." ECCLESIASTES 11:9

"Go ye into all the world and preach the Gospel to every creature." In the same breath, to comfort His children, He said, "Lo, I am with you alway, even unto the end of the world." The disciples to whom He then spoke, have been in His visible presence for hundreds of years, and the world is not yet ended; the comfort lasts yet, and so, therefore, must the commission.

"My heart repeats the promise o'er and o'er,
Though 'tis an 'old, old story' heard before,
Yet with each dear repeating loved the more.
Be lighted from within, by unseen Guest,
Send out warm rays of love to all distrest,
And lure them by your shining into rest."

Do I think you can so love Christ that whatever sacrifices of personal ease or comfort you may make for His sake will become so much a joy as to cease to be claimed under the head of sacrifice? Aye, indeed, there is a higher plane than sacrifice.

"Yet if any man suffer as a Christian, let him not be ashamed; but let him glorify God on this behalf." 1 PETER 4:16

When a sensible person has made a misstep, the thing for him is to undo as much of the mischief as he can; as quickly as he can; it is the *only* way he has of showing the difference between himself and a fool.

"The way of a fool is right in his own eyes: but he that hearkeneth unto counsel is wise."   PROVERBS 12:15
"Hath not God made foolish the wisdom of this world?"
                                        1 CORINTHIANS 1:20

We must guard against a temptation to do evil, that good may come.

"What shall we say then, Shall we continue in sin, that grace may abound?
God forbid. How shall we that are dead to sin, live any longer therein?"
                                        ROMANS 6:1-2

There are a great many sensible people in the world, and the world does not love them at all, and half of the time it is their own foolish fault for being so "cranky" over trifles.

"For ye pay tithe of mint and anise and cummin."
                                        MATTHEW 23:23

If I were to talk with one of my friends who is not acquainted with you, and tell her how kind you were, and how interested in all young people, and how pleasant and helpful you were, it doesn't seem to me that I should prejudice her against you. Why should I feel afraid of prejudicing them against my Saviour?

"Acquaint now thyself with him, and be at peace: thereby good shall come unto thee." JOB 22:21

Knowing that you ought to feel differently, there is just one thing you can do, it is your part; you can give that heart which is full of hard feelings and self-will and bitterness, into the Lord's hands, and tell Him you want it to be made a fit place for him.

"Purge me with hyssop, and I shall be clean: wash me, and I shall be whiter than snow." PSALM 51:7

When I am conversing with any person what is my habitual theme?

"What manner of communications are these that ye have one to another?" LUKE 24:17

How hard it must be for the Great Physician to bear with us in our determination to think of His love and care for us as only a piece of that which He bears for the great multitudes, instead of individualizing it as He constantly teaches us to do, and accepting Him as caring for us with even more of the exclusive tenderness of love which we give to our own.

"I have called thee by thy name; thou art mine." ISAIAH 43:1

MAY

What gorgeous coloring and delicate tracery in the leaves! Does it ever occur to you to wonder that such great skill should have been expended in just making them look pretty to please our eyes?

"Sing unto him, sing psalms unto him: talk ye of all his wondrous works." PSALM 105:2

"Who sweeps a room as for thy law,
Makes that, and the action, fine."

I am glad the grand old author said that. And yet, an older and grander Author said it better: "Whosoever giveth a cup of cold water."

"Thy thoughts are very deep."
PSALM 92:5

What if the Holy Spirit has suggested it, and will give you a message which He knows can reach a stranger, and draw him home?

"Thou gavest also thy good spirit to instruct them." NEHEMIAH 9:20

And you think that Jesus Christ has nothing to do with the black kettle, and the boiler, or the sink, or a dozen other things with which you will come in contact to-day? That is such a mistake. Remember it is He who said, "Whether therefore ye eat, or drink, or *whatsoever* ye do, do all to the glory of God."

"For your heavenly Father knoweth that ye have need of all these things." MATTHEW 6:32

Justified! Not because I have done right; not because my judgment is correct; not because of any act of mine in any direction save that one of trusting in my Lord, justified by *faith!*

"Therefore being justified by faith, we have peace with God through our Lord Jesus Christ." ROMANS 5:1

What should you conclude as to Christian duty in the matter of daily conversation?

"But as he which hath called you is holy, so be ye holy in all manner of conversation." 1 PETER 1:15

It is a strange thing, but how can we help believing it to be actually the case, that people who would be shocked at the idea of violating their word given to their fellow-men yet seem to ignore, without much trouble of conscience, the most solemn obligation made to God!

"Take heed unto yourselves, lest you forget the covenant of the Lord your God."   DEUTERONOMY 4:23

MAY 8TH

There is a sunlight so high and strong that the clouds of this world cannot reach it.

"But ye are a chosen generation, a royal priesthood, a holy nation, a peculiar people; that ye should shew forth the praises of him who hath called you out of darkness into his marvelous light."   1 PETER 2:9

MAY 9TH

I try to remember that Christ knows it all, and he loves me, and he is all-powerful; and yet he leads me through this dark road; therefore it *must* be right.

"Nevertheless the foundation of God standeth sure, having this seal, The Lord knoweth them that are his."   2 TIMOTHY 2:19

MAY 10TH

He will not come into a divided heart; a heart which says, "In some things I will obey; but in this, and this, and this, I must have my own way."

You would not expect even a human friend who had the right to direct you, to accept such a position as that, would you? How much less the Lord?

"No man can serve two masters: for either he will hate the one and love the other; or else he will hold to the one and despise the other. Ye cannot serve God and mammon." MATTHEW 6:24

MAY 11TH

I believe that religion should have sufficient power over us to change all our tastes and plans in life, fitting them to the Saviour's use.

"That Christ may dwell in your hearts by faith; that ye, being rooted and grounded in love,
May be able to comprehend with all saints what is the breadth, and length, and depth, and height;
And to know the love of Christ which passeth knowledge, that ye might be filled with all the fullness of God." EPHESIANS 3:17

MAY 12TH

One could not live long in this world without realizing the forcefulness of the sentence: "Every heart knoweth its own bitterness." Behind the sunniest, apparently most enviable life, the bitterness hides.

"When thou passest through the waters, I will be with thee: when thou walkest through the fire, thou shalt not be burned; neither shall the flame kindle upon thee." ISAIAH 43:2

MAY 13TH

Will you open the door for Jesus to come in, by telling Him that your heart is all wrong, and you want it made right? Just as you would tell me, if I had assured you that I was both able and willing to do *all* the rest for you.

"And the Lord direct your hearts into the love of God, and into the patient waiting for Christ." 2 THESSALONIANS 3:5

MAY 14TH

Are these too small for His notice, when He Himself refers us to the fading wild flowers for lessons?

"The grass withereth, and the flower thereof falleth away:
But the word of the Lord endureth forever." ISAIAH 40:8

MAY 15TH

He sees the way plainly and He will lead us right through the thickets to the sunlight of his eternal presence.

"But there the glorious Lord will be to us a place of broad rivers and streams; wherein shall no galley with oars, neither shall gallant ships pass thereby." ISAIAH 33:21

MAY 16TH

I really believe that the Lord, when He said, "Give, and it shall be given unto you, good measure, pressed down and shaken together, and running over, shall men give into your bosom," meant just what he said.

"There hath not failed one word of all his good promise."
1 KINGS 8:56

"She impresses me as one who is being led; who does not choose to go alone, has not learned how, indeed. A very few Christians never learn how, and with them the Lord does his special work."

"The secret of the Lord is with them that fear him; and he will show them his covenant." PSALM 25:14

There may be loneliness and a reaching out after, and sometimes an unutterable longing for the morning, but to those who are sure, *sure* beyond the possibility of a doubt, that the eternal morning *will* dawn, and dawn for them, there is never again a desolation.

"Weeping may endure for a night, but joy cometh in the morning." PSALM 30:5

It is God's world, and He made your little children. You may be sure He has a place for them, both in this world and in Heaven.

"Fear not, little flock; for it is your Father's good pleasure to give you the kingdom." LUKE 12:32

Oh! to know for a certainty whether some who have a name to live, are really alive; and so be at rest about them.

"I have no greater joy than to hear that my children walk in truth."

3 JOHN 1:4

She envied their free and easy life, without a care to harass them, as it seemed to her.

If she had but thought, she had a robe, and a crown, and a harp, and a place waiting for her, up before the throne of God; and all they had *not*.

"Henceforth there is laid up for me a crown of righteousness, which the Lord, the righteous judge, shall give me at that day: and not to me only, but unto all them also that love his appearing."   2 TIMOTHY 4:8

If God from his infinite height, can look down upon all the world, having the same wonderful, patient, persistent love for all mankind, what am I that I should not give my utmost strength for the poorest and meanest of His creatures?

"For if there come into your assembly a man with a gold ring, in goodly apparel, and there come in also a poor man in vile raiment;

And ye have respect to him that weareth the gay clothing, and say unto him, Sit thou here in a good place; and say to the poor, Stand thou there, or sit here under my footstool: Are ye not then partial in yourselves, and are become judges of evil thoughts?"   JAMES 2:3

We are all set apart, given to Him to use as He will. The trouble is that so many of us take back the gifts, and use our time and our tongues as though they were our own.

". . . Ye are not your own?"

"For ye are bought with a price: therefore glorify God in your body, and in your spirit, which are God's." 1 Corinthians 6:19-20

May 24th

A thing that can possibly lead one to eternal death, a Christian has no business to meddle with, even if he knows of but one soul in a million years that has been so wrecked.

"And through thy knowledge shall the weak brother perish, for whom Christ died?" 1 Corinthians 8:11

May 25th

I am not giving my own money; it is His, and He lets me spend it on His work. If it were mine I might be tempted to spend it on myself; but since it belongs to Him, of course it is a mere act of common honesty to give it back to Him.

"The silver is mine, and the gold is mine, saith the Lord of Hosts." Haggai 2:8

May 26th

Isn't it a pity in this carping world we cannot oftener put ourselves in other people's places, mentally, at least, and try to discover how we should probably feel, and talk, and act, were we surrounded by their circumstances and biased by their educations?

"Rejoice with them that do rejoice, and weep with them that weep." Romans 12:15

When we do not see the way clearly; when we are beset with difficulties; when disappointments thicken around us, we can still look up to God and say, "Up there, where Father is, it is peace."

"And the peace of God, which passeth all understanding, shall keep your hearts and minds through Christ Jesus."　　PHILIPPIANS 4:7

It would be a pity to get ready for only one world when the other is so near by.

"Provide yourself bags which wax not old, a treasure in the heavens that faileth not, where no thief approacheth, neither moth corrupteth."　　LUKE 12:33

We are at work for immortal *souls*. Think of it! they *must* live forever. Shall they, through all eternity, keep dropping lower and lower, or shall they wear crowns?

"And many of them that sleep in the dust of the earth shall awake, some to everlasting life, and some to shame and everlasting contempt."　　DANIEL 12:2

It is the trifling sacrifices that pinch. One can do a great thing now and then, that he knows people will admire, even though he has no such selfish motive in doing it, still it helps and cheers, to know that an appreciative world looks on and says: "That was well done!" But to go without a new dress all winter — to go to church, and to society, and occasionally to a tea-party, wearing the cashmere or alpaca that has done duty as best for two years, and do it for the sake of the church, and say nothing about it, and know that people are ignorant of the reason, and feel that they are wondering whether you are aware that your dress begins to look "rusty" — that is sacrifice.

"She shall be brought unto the king in raiment of needlework."
PSALM 45:14

MAY 31ST

You speak the truth earnestly, forcibly, and with strong common sense on your side, but the verse says, "speaking the truth in love." And don't you know that that part of it you have a way of keeping hidden in your heart, so that the truth sometimes wounds where you would have it heal?

"By pureness, by knowledge, by longsuffering, by kindness, by the Holy Ghost, by love unfeigned." 2 CORINTHIANS 6:6

JUNE

Some of our dear Christian ladies have but just heard a faint echo of His call, "Go ye into all the world," though it has been sounding for centuries. There are many of them standing now on the threshold, dazed with the echo, scarcely knowing if it can possibly mean them, and seeing sacrifice and burden where one day they will "count it all joy."

> *"I dare not work my soul to save,*
> *That work my Lord has done;*
> *But I will work like any slave*
> *For the love of God's dear Son."*

Graves seem to me hard things to leave. People who are alive, and from whom I can hear, and to whom I can write long letters, are different; but, someway, one holds on to graves and wants to be near them.

> *"Then the disciples went away unto their own home. But Mary stood without at the sepulchre weeping: and as she wept, she stooped down, and looked into the sepulchre."* JOHN 20:11

I wonder if people realize that they can arrange flowers in such a manner as to glorify the Lord of the garden.

"Let my beloved come into his garden."   SONG OF SOLOMON 4:16

Just think of that ivy, it would have grown as rapidly and been quite as healthy if the leaves had been square, and all of them an intense green, instead of being shaded into that lovely dark scalloped border all around the outer edge.

"O Lord, how manifold are thy works! in wisdom hast thou made them all: the earth is full of thy riches."   PSALM 104:24

It seems blessed to think that the Lord Jesus took such minute notice of our human nature that he knew it would help us to be allowed to keep a subject constantly before Him, and to keep coaxing about it.

"I say unto you, Though he will not rise and give him, because he is his friend, yet because of his importunity he will rise and give him as many as he needeth."   LUKE 11:8

The Lord sees the heart; and little seeds of loving kindness to one's neighbor, whether he be next door or across the ocean, may be in many hearts, unknown to us.

"For the Lord searcheth all hearts, and understandeth all the imaginations of the thoughts." 1 CHRONICLES 28:9

JUNE 7TH

I have often looked forward to an evening gathering with eager interest and thankfulness, because of the opportunity for meeting some there whom I could not catch elsewhere and saying a word for my Master.

"In the morning sow thy seed, and in the evening withhold not thine hand: for thou knowest not whether shall prosper, either this or that, or whether they both shall be alike good." ECCLESIASTES 11:6

JUNE 8TH

Was it possible that the Divine Physician saw her need of such bitter herbs as these which had fallen to her lot?

"As many as I love, I rebuke and chasten; be zealous, therefore, and repent." REVELATION 3:19

JUNE 9TH

You and I know and feel that we must give an account of our stewardship. Do you see how people who ask God to help them in every little thing which they have to decide — in the least expenditure of money — can after that deliberately fritter it away?

"So then every one of us shall give account of himself to God." ROMANS 14:12

The heart of Christ is for each, as if each were alone in all the world the object of His care.

"Yet will I not forget thee." ISAIAH 49:15

It was pitiful to see how she clung to her poor little rag that she had called religion, and felt as though if she should actually let go and say, "I am not a Christian," it would be a settled doom to her, and yet — how could it be that she knew anything experimentally about this matter, to have lived the life she had?

"I know thy works, that thou hast a name that thou livest, and art dead." REVELATION 3:1

Do you think that Christians whose rule of life reads "Whatsoever ye do, do all to the glory of God," have any right to go to social gatherings, or anywhere else, separated from this end?

"In all thy ways acknowledge him, and he shall direct thy paths." PROVERBS 3:6

Didn't you give Him your tongue when you gave Him yourself? And yet you are fortunate if you have not dishonored Him with it many a time.

"Be not rash with thy mouth, and let not thine heart be hasty to utter anything before God: for God is in heaven, and thou upon earth: therefore let thy words be few."   ECCLESIASTES 5:2

JUNE 14TH

It is easier to do things which you like, and which in a sense are natural to you, than it is to do what goes utterly against the selfish side of your nature.

"For all seek their own, not the things which are Jesus Christ's."
PHILIPPIANS 2:21

JUNE 15TH

"Who shall roll us away the stone?" They worried a great deal about that stone, how they would get it rolled away, and when they got there it was gone. I'll remember that; when I see a stone ahead of me I won't stop and fret about it; I'll walk straight up to it, and when I get there maybe it will roll out of my way.

"The angel of the Lord descended from heaven, and came and rolled back the stone from the door, and sat upon it."   MATTHEW 28:2

JUNE 16TH

They aren't worth lifting a finger for. And yet, how can I help remembering that if the Lord Jesus had said that of us, and stayed up there in His glory, we should have been utterly without help or hope to-day?

"For scarcely for a righteous man will one die: yet peradventure for a good man some would even dare to die.

But God commendeth his love toward us, in that, while we were yet sinners, Christ died for us."   ROMANS 5:7

"He maketh the wrath of man to praise him."
I suppose He can make the blunderings of men, and of women, too, do the same. We must just leave it with *Him*, and try again.

"Who shall change our vile body, that it may be fashioned like unto his glorious body, according to the working whereby he is able even to subdue all things unto himself."   PHILIPPIANS 3:21

An awakened conscience toyed with, is a very fruitful source of misery.

"And herein do I exercise myself, to have always a conscience void of offence toward God, and toward men."   ACTS 24:16

I bless Him that I may constantly serve, whether I am wiping the dust from my table, or whether I am on my knees.

"With good will, doing service, as to the Lord, and not to men."
                                                            EPHESIANS 6:7

"My grace is sufficient," not for my saints only — those who have been faithful and successful — but for *thee*.

"Fear thou not; for I am with thee: be not dismayed; for I am thy God: I will strengthen thee; yea, I will help thee; yea, I will uphold thee with the right hand of my righteousness." ISAIAH 41:10

I doubt whether we should wait always for clear ways; perhaps we are expected to go creeping along in the dark. Satan has ways, and doesn't scruple to use them.

"For I the Lord thy God will hold thy right hand, saying unto thee, Fear not; I will help thee." ISAIAH 41:13

"Leaving us an example, that ye should follow his steps." The true pattern is certainly perfect; why not follow that? Who ever asks the schoolboy to imitate the scrawl of some fellow pupil, so long as the perfect copy is just before his eyes, at the top of the page?

"Be ye followers of God, as dear children." EPHESIANS 5:1

Nothing that you or I can do can possibly make one sin white, one mistake as though it had not been, give one moment of rest to a troubled heart. But the blood of Jesus Christ can do all this.

"The blood of Jesus Christ his Son cleanseth us from all sin."
1 JOHN 1:7

She did not realize the feeling, and yet she possessed somewhat of the same spirit of the child who prayed: "Dear Jesus, help me to be good to-day. I know I can be good if I try, and I intend to try, but you can help me if you want to!"

"For thou, Lord, only makest me dwell in safety."   PSALM 4:8

I have met people who, it seemed to me, would rather trust their "rainy day fund" than the Lord.

"If I have made gold my hope, or have said to the fine gold, Thou art my confidence: This also were an iniquity to be punished by the judge; for I should have denied the God that is above."   JOB 31:24

I should never have dared to assume the cares and responsibilities of our home if I had not known that I could go to Christ for direction as to how to wisely spend the money He put into my hands, and how to order all my affairs so that there would be no friction.

"Cast thy burden upon the Lord, and he shall sustain thee: he shall never suffer the righteous to be moved."   PSALM 55:22

The veriest child can be a witness if he knows any thing about the facts; and I do certainly know some wonderful things about Jesus to which I could witness; and besides, isn't it reasonable to suppose that He will appear to me every day with things for me to witness to?

"I have appeared unto thee for this purpose, to make thee a minister and a witness, both of these things which thou hast seen, and of those things in which I will appear unto thee."   ACTS 26:16

Rewards for petty sacrifices are often so slow to come that it is not uncommon for lives to pass out into the future without receiving a word or glance of recompense. But there are occasional other experiences.

"Therefore, my beloved brethren, be ye steadfast, unmovable, always abounding in the work of the Lord, for as much as ye know that your labor is not in vain in the Lord."   1 CORINTHIANS 15:58

It is a question whether we have any right to indulge in an amusement that has the power to lead people astray, especially when it is impossible to tell what boy may be growing up under that influence to whom it will become a snare.

"It is good neither to eat flesh, nor to drink wine, nor anything whereby thy brother stumbleth, or is offended, or is made weak."

ROMANS 14:21

You mustn't quarrel with the Lord's plans of work, until you understand more about them. By the way, I presume He has a plan for *you* to work by, that you have never so much as looked into. It is a subject entirely worthy of your consideration.

"But know that the Lord hath set apart him that is godly for himself."

PSALM 4:3

JULY

Your soul, remember, was worth the death of the Son of God. See that you make your life worthy such a sacrifice as that.

"For as much as ye know that ye were not redeemed with corruptible things, as silver and gold, from your vain conversation received by tradition from your fathers;
But with the precious blood of Christ, as of a lamb without blemish and without spot." 1 PETER 1:18

It cannot be possible that you think when a waiting soul asks you to pray, Christ does not say to you, "Do it"?

"And it shall be, if he call thee, that thou shalt say, Speak, Lord; for thy servant heareth." 1 SAMUEL 3:19

"Girls, we have spent our strength vainly. It is our privilege to get up higher; to look at all these things from the mount whereon

God will let us stand, if we want to climb."

"Therefore leaving the principles of the doctrine of Christ, let us go on unto perfection." HEBREWS 6:1

JULY 4TH

There is no trade on earth so easy to learn as grumbling.

"Bless the Lord, O my soul, and forget not all his benefits." PSALM 103:2

JULY 5TH

I couldn't doubt my right. Indeed it seemed to me to be a duty, not only to pray, but actually to supplicate, to coax, you know, just as I was so tempted to do when a child.

"In everything by prayer and supplication with thanksgiving let your requests be made known unto God." PHILIPPIANS 4:6

JULY 6TH

I pity the man who has not brain power enough, and insight into the future enough, to be willing to be anchored in God.

"And I will say unto my soul, Soul, thou hast much goods laid up for many years; take thine ease, eat, drink, and be merry.
But God said unto him, Thou fool, this night thy soul shall be required of thee: then whose shall those things be, which thou hast provided?" LUKE 12:19

I shall have to confess that Ruth's old obstinacy came to her aid; — or to her hinderance, as you will; concessions which she could have made, she would not; and when she might have resisted gently, gracefully, she often did it sternly, with a determination to carry her point, which was much more evident to her husband than was the reason for carrying it.

"And the servant of the Lord must not strive; but be gentle unto all men, apt to teach, patient." 2 TIMOTHY 2:24

You have left the duty of *giving* subject to the accident of having something left after all your wants are supplied. Is that really the way?

"And of all that thou shalt give me I will surely give the tenth unto thee." GENESIS 28:22

Will He not be pleased with even my little bits of efforts if He knows that my sincere desire is to save souls for his glory?

"And every man shall receive his own reward according to his own labor." 1 CORINTHIANS 3:8

No one ever was afraid of becoming a drunkard. If people only were afraid, we should have no drunkards.

"Wherefore let him that thinketh he standeth take heed lest he fall."
1 CORINTHIANS 10:12

JULY 11TH

We must feel some little measure of the same love for a soul, that the Lord Jesus does when he calls after it, else how can we hope to reach it?

"And that He died for all, that they which live should not henceforth live unto themselves, but unto Him which died for them, and rose again."
2 CORINTHIANS 5:15

JULY 12TH

It always seemed to me a bad sign to see people amused with caricatures of good, pure *old* faces.

"And as he was going up by the way, there came forth little children out of the city, and mocked him, and said unto him, Go up, thou bald head; go up, thou bald head.
And he turned back, and looked on them, and cursed them in the name of the Lord."
2 KINGS 2:23-24

JULY 13TH

It was such a lovely Sunday morning! The world looked just as glad and happy as a world can look. The church bells seemed like joyful music; that is, they sounded so to some people. What a pity that people and things can not be in tune in this world.

"I was glad when they said unto me, Let us go into the house of the Lord.

Our feet shall stand within thy gates, O Jerusalem.

Jerusalem is builded as a city that is compact together:

Whither the tribes go up, the tribes of the Lord, unto the testimony of Israel, to give thanks unto the name of the Lord." PSALM 122:1

JULY 14TH

Alas for the Christian world which believes in theory, that there is a direct link between the seen and the unseen, by which the earnest soul can be told in what way to walk, and, in practice, thinks it must search out its own way!

"O thou of little faith, wherefore didst thou doubt?"
MATTHEW 14:31

JULY 15TH

"You know, mamma, you trained us to a very careful attention to fashion, in all its details; we want to do full justice to your early teachings. As Madame Dupont used to say, 'A young lady who is not *au fait* in all that regards the demands of fashion, is dead already.' " It was a keen, pointed arrow, and it struck home. Ruth sat and thought about it after she was left alone; as she had sat and thought many a day, since her work for these girls began to develop in ways of which she had not dreamed.

"Ye shall know them by their fruits. Do men gather grapes of thorns, or figs of thistles?"
MATTHEW 7:16

JULY 16TH

"There is no desolation of heart to those who part at night to meet again in the morning."

"He will swallow up death in victory; the Lord God will wipe away tears from off all faces; and the rebuke of his people shall he take away from off all the earth: for the Lord hath spoken it." ISAIAH 25:8

JULY 17TH

When the church and the world start out to walk hand in hand, it is a curious thing that it is always the world that sees the inconsistencies, and laughs, and always the church that is blind.

"Wherefore come out from among them, and be ye separate, saith the Lord." 2 CORINTHIANS 6:17

"Then the Church sat down at her ease and said: 'I am rich and in goods increased.
I have need of nothing and naught to do,
    But to laugh, and dance, and feast.'
But the sly world heard her, and laughed in his sleeve,
    And mockingly said, aside,
'The church has fallen, the beautiful church,
    And her shame is her boast and pride.' "

JULY 18TH

I have known kitchens that ought to have glowed with the beauty of the strong unselfish hearts beating there through danger, and trial, and harassing toil.

"To them who by patient continuance in well doing seek for glory and honor and immortality, eternal life." ROMANS 2:7

JULY 19TH

More things than some people dream of, are going on in this world of ours.

"And Jacob awaked out of his sleep, and he said, Surely the Lord is in this place; and I knew it not."   GENESIS 28:16

Sunday is a blessed day of rest; and to think that the Lord gives a wonderful promise to them that keep it!

"If thou turn away thy foot from the sabbath, from doing thy pleasure on my holy day; and call the sabbath a delight, the holy of the Lord, honorable; and shalt honor him, not doing thine own ways, nor finding thine own pleasure, nor speaking thine own words:

Then shalt thou delight thyself in the Lord; and I will cause thee to ride upon the high places of the earth, and feed thee with the heritage of Jacob thy father: for the mouth of the Lord hath spoken it."   ISAIAH 58:13

It is a fearful thing for one who loves the Lord to move about under the Satan-inflicted torture of the thought: "He is cruel: He is cruel!"

"In all this Job sinned not, nor charged God foolishly."   JOB 1:22

A boy would be thought insane who would laugh at another for trying to save his life, or to save himself from being hurt in any way; but, because one wants to save his soul, wants him to act like a creature who is to live forever, and can be happy or wretched just as he pleases, then some are ready to laugh. Is such folly worth minding?

"Whosoever therefore shall be ashamed of me and of my words; of him also shall the Son of man be ashamed, when he cometh in the glory of his Father with the holy angels." MARK 8:3

JULY 23RD

I suppose Paul made failures, but he thought that Christ's blood was powerful enough to atone for even failures, and His love strong enough to forgive them. I don't imagine that Paul kept looking back and sighing over them after Christ had forgiven them. Do you?

"Forgetting those things which are behind, and reaching forth unto those things which are before,
I press toward the mark for the prize of the high calling of God in Christ Jesus." PHILIPPIANS 3:1

JULY 24T

There is at least that amount of comfort to be gotten out of a disagreeable duty faithfully performed — the performer, by the time the work is done, has generally reached a higher plane of life where he can say: "I followed the path pointed out as nearly as I could. The results are not for me to arrange. The matter has been handed over to the Master's hands."

"And Moses went up from the plains of Moab unto the mountain Nebo, to the top of Pisgah, that is over against Jericho. And the Lord shewed him all the land of Gilead, unto Dan. . . . . And the Lord said unto him, This is the land which I sware unto Abraham, unto Isaac, and unto Jacob, saying, I will give it unto thy seed: I have caused thee to see with thine eyes." DEUTERONOMY 34:1,

Do you think we ought to have an "anything but that," between the Lord and our prayers?

"And he went away again the second time, and prayed, saying, O my Father, if this cup may not pass away from me, except I drink it, thy will be done." MATTHEW 26:42

To what use could those large silent rooms be put which would reflect honor on the One to whom all hers was consecrated? Ah, therein lay the secret of the difficulty! She must say "our rooms," if only she could say, "all *ours* is consecrated," how plainly would the answer to this painful riddle glow before her! She knew a dozen beautiful things that might be done with cultured *consecrated* homes.

"Can two walk together, except they be agreed?" AMOS 3:3

One reason why our friends are not converted is because we, their leaders, walk so crookedly that we keep them all the time stumbling over us.

"Can the blind lead the blind? shall they not both fall into the ditch?" LUKE 6:39

Where would be the church of Christ without its living, working members?

"Thou hast a few names even in Sardis which have not defiled their garments; and they shall walk with me in white: for they are worthy."
REVELATION 3:4

JULY 29TH

Don't allow yourself for one moment to limit the power and the grace of a Saviour. Remember he is "mighty to save."

"Now unto him that is able to do exceeding aboundantly above all that we ask or think, according to the power that worketh in us;
Unto him be glory in the Church by Jesus Christ throughout all ages, world without end."
EPHESIANS 3:20

JULY 30TH

I wonder how I should feel if I should go to heaven and meet one of those whom I ought to have known in the church on earth, and the Lord should see that we were strangers!

"Now therefore ye are no more strangers and foreigners, but fellow-citizens with the saints, and of the household of God." EPHESIANS 2:19

JULY 31ST

The fact is, we must learn to work for Christ, and not set up business for ourselves, and still expect Him to give the wages.

"He that is not with me is against me; and he that gathereth not with me scattereth abroad."
MATTHEW 12:30

AUGUST

So many things in this world squeak for the want of a thoughtful hand to administer a drop of oil.

"To appoint unto them that mourn in Zion, to give unto them beauty for ashes, the oil of joy for mourning, the garment of praise for the spirit of heaviness; that they might be called trees of righteousness, the planting of the Lord, that he might be glorified."   ISAIAH 61:3

If it were wise or kind to make such distinctions I could wish that those whose friends have gone, without a gleam of light, into an unknown future, should wear the crêpe and bombazine; and let us, who have seen the reflection of the glory signalize it by wearing only dazzling white.

"And to her was granted that she should be arrayed in fine linen, clean and white: for the fine linen is the righteousness of saints."   REVELATION 19:8

"I ain't one that expects folks sixteen years old to act as though they was sixty," said Mrs. Smith.

"When I was a child, I spake as a child, I understood as a child, I thought as a child: but when I became a man I put away childish things." 1 CORINTHIANS 13:11

We are almost tired of all sorts of books, but there is one Book which never wears out. What if you and I should begin to study the Bible?

"How sweet are thy words unto my taste! yea, sweeter than honey to my mouth!" PSALM 119:103

When I remember the infinite height above us all that the Lord occupies, and how He *stoops*, to have anything to do with one of us, I am humiliated at the idea of calling any work of mine lowly. There are times when there seems to me no very great heights or depths of humanity.

"Hearken, my beloved brethren, Hath not God chosen the poor of this world rich in faith, and heirs of the kingdom which he hath promised to them that love him?" JAMES 2:5

I can't help feeling that you are planning in your own heart just what ought to be done, and then allowing yourself to feel almost indignant and ill-used because the work is not accomplished.

"For as the heavens are higher than the earth, so are my ways higher than your ways, and my thoughts than your thoughts." ISAIAH 55:9

Oh! there were constant blunders which this poor blundering Christian made. She needed helping from the human side; and she had chosen a broken reed to lean upon. Is it any wonder that she made mistakes? I am not excusing her. She might, even under these circumstances, have gone to the Stronghold, and received grace sufficient. What I am saying, is, that she made life harder for herself than it need have been.

"Be ye not unequally yoked together with unbelievers: for what fellowship hath righteousness with unrighteousness? and what communion hath light with darkness?" 2 CORINTHIANS 6:14

There is a way of praying about a soul with whom we are offended — or, at least, we call it praying — which is simply pouring out one's knowledge of that person's shortcomings in a most vindictive way before the One whom we almost unconsciously feel ought to come to our help and administer rebuke.

"And when ye stand praying, forgive, if ye have ought against any: that your Father also which is in heaven may forgive you your trespasses." MARK 11:25

I wonder when the Lord's own people will awaken to the fact that there are no trivial things in life? that there are no passing moments but what decide the eternal destinies of souls?

"Thou tellest my wanderings: put thou my tears into thy bottle: are they not in thy book?"   PSALM 56:8

God is on your side, He will surely deliver you if you trust in Him; if you turn from Him how can He help you?

"Except these abide in the ship, ye cannot be saved."   ACTS 27:3

You will find that if this life is a warfare we have more than a Captain — we've a Commander-in-chief, and we have nothing to do with the fight, other than to obey orders and keep behind the shield.

"Looking unto Jesus the author and finisher of our faith."
HEBREWS 12:2

Meantime where was Satan? Content to let this reaping time alone? Oh! bless you, no. Never busier, never more alert, and watchful, and cautious, and skillful than now. It was wonderful, too, how many helpers he found whose names were actually on the roll of the Church!

"Satan hath desired to have you."   LUKE 22:31

Those girls had climbed; they were standing — at least so far as these trying little beginnings of religious experience were concerned, away above them — troubled by them no more.

"For which cause we faint not; but though our outward man perish, yet the inward man is renewed day by day."   2 CORINTHIANS 4:16

When you accepted Christ as your Friend, did you not engage to take *some* things on trust — to believe that what *you* could not *see*, was yet clear to the eye and the heart of your Saviour, and that He ruled?

"Jesus saith unto him, Thomas, because thou hast seen me, thou hast believed: blessed are they that have not seen, and yet have believed."
                                                                JOHN 20:29

There is just One who fought a battle with Satan and came off victor, and there never will be another. The victory must come through Him, or it is at best a very partial, and at all times a doubtful one. In Him are safety and everlasting strength, and outside of Him is danger.

"Then the devil leaveth him, and, behold, angels came and ministered unto him."   MATTHEW 4:11

How wonderful that any of us are careless or thoughtless for a *moment,* so long as we have a child or a friend unsafe.

"Brethren, my heart's desire and prayer to God for Israel is, that th[ey]
might be saved." ROMANS 10[:1]

She had prayed for it, but she was like many another Christi[an]
worker in that she had not seemed to expect the answer to h[er]
prayer. Verily, He has to be content with exceeding little faith.

"But let him ask in faith, nothing wavering. For be that wavereth [is]
like a wave of the sea driven with the wind and tossed." JAMES 1[:6]

"If I prefer not Jerusalem above my chief joy," what then? Wh[y]
then I am false to my covenant vows, and the possibilities are tha[t I]
am none of His.

> *"Beyond my highest joy*
> *I prize her heavenly ways;*
> *Her sweet communion, solemn vows,*
> *Her hymns of love and praise."*

A religious uplifting which does not bubble over into whatever pr[ac]-
tical work the heart or the hands find to do, is not apt to continue.

"Therefore they that were scattered abroad went everywhere preachi[ng]
the word." ACTS 8[:4]

"Here was she, after the lapse of years, sitting beside the one with whom she had spent the most of them, and he had gotten no farther than the old, worn-out query: "Wherein lies the harm?" The solemn question was, Did this tell something of her own spiritual state?

"For when for the time ye ought to be teachers, ye have need that one teach you again which be the first principles of the oracles of God; and are become such as have need of milk, and not of strong meat."　　　　　HEBREWS 5:12

God bless the souls who, capable of rising to the heights which belong to immortality, yet think of kitchen fires and breakfasts.

"Wherefore I pray you to take some meat: for this is for your health: for there shall not an hair fall from the head of any of you."

"And when Paul had gathered a bundle of sticks, and laid them on the fire, there came a viper out of the heat, and fastened on his hand. . . . And he shook off the beast into the fire, and felt no harm."　　　ACTS 27:34;
28:3, 5

Dear, half-asleep Christian, wonders are taking place all about you, and is it possible that you are merely engaged in trying to prove to yourself and others that "the age of miracles is past"? though why you should be very anxious to prove it, does not clearly appear even to yourself.

"What meanest thou, O sleeper? arise, call upon thy God."
JONAH 1:6

So long as the Lord said there was a place by Him, and promised to hide us, and promised to shield us, and promised to cover us with His hands, and promised to gather us under His wings, why should we be forever starting off alone, or at best only allowing Him to push a little, while we go ahead and climb?

"He that dwelleth in the secret place of the most High shall abide under the shadow of the Almighty." PSALM 91:1

A band of young people plunged heart and soul into anything, are almost certain to succeed. The everlasting pity is that so often success is not worth the price paid.

"Then I looked on all the works that my hands had wrought, and on the labour that I had laboured to do: and, behold, all was vanity and vexation of spirit, and there was no profit under the sun." ECCLESIASTES 2:11

There is many a boy who coaxes a girl to go where he wishes in his soul she may have Christian firmness to refuse.

"If sinners entice thee, consent thou not." PROVERBS 1:10

We shall probably never know, on this side, how far the prayers of the mothers at home reach.

"And it came to pass, as she continued praying before the Lord, that Eli marked her mouth.

Now Hannah, she spake in her heart; only her lips moved, but her voice was not heard." 1 SAMUEL 1:12

AUGUST 27TH

I think sometimes our Heavenly Father does just as we do with the children. He lets us stumble in a place where it is not too hard, so that we will learn what it is to obey.

"Except ye be converted, and become as little children, ye shall not enter into the kingdom of heaven." MATTHEW 18:3

AUGUST 28TH

The Lord knows you; knows just what place He has set you in; just how many people you can touch with your influence, and just what He is going to do with them all.

"The Lord thy God hath chosen thee." DEUTERONOMY 7:6

AUGUST 29TH

"Get thee behind me, Satan." The only perfect Life gave that sentence once, not alone for Himself; thank God, He has many a time since enabled His weak children of the flesh to repeat it in triumph.

"Resist the devil, and he will flee from you." JAMES 4:7

How wonderful will the revelations of Heaven be, when certain, whose lives have touched for a few days and then separated, shall meet, in some of the cycles of eternity, and talk things over!

"And it came to pass, that the beggar died, and was carried by the angels into Abraham's bosom."　　　　　　　　LUKE 16:22

Poor Ruth was destined to realize fully that one may shut the doors with emphasis against tangible guests, and yet receive a whole troop of miscreants into one's heart, who made havoc with holy time.

"Keep thy heart with all diligence; for out of it are the issues of life."
PROVERBS 4:23

SEPTEMBER

In that glorious old prophet's book is my jubilant verse: —
"And the ransomed of the Lord shall return, and come to Zion
with songs and everlasting joy upon their heads: they shall obtain
joy and gladness, and sorrow and sighing shall flee away."

> *"Oh! sweet and blessed Country,*
> *The home of God's elect;*
> *Oh! sweet and blessed Country,*
> *That eager hearts expect;*
> *Jesus, in mercy bring us*
> *To that dear land of rest;*
> *Who art, with God the Father,*
> *And Spirit, ever blest."*

When one attempts not only to drop the seed, but to make the
fruit that shall spring up, no wonder one stands back appalled!

"I have planted, Apollos watered; but God gave the increase."
1 CORINTHIANS 3:6

There is a sense in which we are all of us unworthy of Christ's love or care, but we are always to remember this: that He has chosen us for His own, that we have been bought with a price, that we are held as infinitely precious in His sight, and that, therefore, we must set a high estimate on our own importance, and live accordingly.

"Since thou wast precious in my sight, thou hast been honorable; and I have loved thee: therefore will I give men for thee, and people for thy life."
ISAIAH 43:4

Reason, being allowed once more to take her seat, accused this Christian woman of having yielded, not to conscience, but to rage. Herein lay the real point of the sting: she knew her action would be attributed to her religion, when she herself realized only too well, that it was the outburst of a moment's ungovernable indignation.

"The heart is deceitful above all things, and desperately wicked: who can know it?" JEREMIAH 17:9

I can't help thinking that there are some people who have not received the Holy Ghost, even though they do believe; not that He hasn't come to them, you know, but that they won't receive Him.

"But the Comforter, which is the Holy Ghost, whom the Father will send in my name, he shall teach you all things, and bring all things to your remembrance, whatsoever I have said unto you." JOHN 14:26

"I have made up my mind that living a Christian life, isn't walking on a feather bed, whether you live in a palace, or a fourth-rate boarding-house, and teach school. I shouldn't wonder if there were such things as vexations everywhere."

"For our light affliction, which is but for a moment, worketh for us a far more exceeding and eternal weight of glory." 2 CORINTHIANS 4:17

Utter shipwreck of human happiness is rarely, thank God, a necessity; even though grievous blunders have been made.

"Return unto me, and I will return unto you, saith the Lord of Hosts." MALACHI 3:7

"That's for all the world like some folks!" Mrs. Solomon Smith remarked meditatively, resting her knitting-needle on her lip and staring into the glow on the hearth. "You have to give them an awful poke, every now and then, before they set themselves to amounting to anything."

"This second epistle, beloved, I now write unto you; in both which I stir up your pure minds by way of remembrance." 2 PETER 3:1

Life is full of victories, and so long as we have a sure Captain to carry on the warfare, and *know* there will be victories, why should we be so disturbed about it?

"But thanks to God, which giveth us the victory through our Lord Jesus Christ."
1 CORINTHIANS 15:57

If you belong to the Lord Jesus, surely He has work for you, and is able to point it out, and to fill your heart with satisfaction while you do His bidding.

"Having then gifts differing according to the grace that is given to us, whether prophecy, let us prophesy according to the proportion of faith."
ROMANS 12:6

Meantime, she slowly made the changes in her dress that had been called for; this much she could do. She smiled somewhat curiously over the discovery that her recent experience had made her look at even so trivial a thing as this, in a new light. Yesterday she would have said that she was sorry her dress did not suit, but as it was the most appropriate garment she had for the occasion, she must ask him to be content with it. To-day, such a response looked humiliatingly hateful. Had she really been a disagreeable Christian through all these years?

"Let this mind be in you, which was also in Christ Jesus."
PHILIPPIANS 2:5

It is a truth that a certain class of Christian workers need to ponder deeply, that when we have done our best, according to the measure of our opportunities, we may safely leave the Holy Spirit to supplement our work.

"Not by might, nor by power, but by my spirit, saith the Lord of Hosts." ZECHARIAH 4:6

There are two ways of keeping a promise; one is to make an attempt and fail, saying to our contented consciences, "There! I've done my duty, and it is no use, you see"; and the other is to persist in attempt after attempt, until the very pertinacity of our faith accomplishes the work for us.

"Moreover it is required in stewards, that a man be found faithful." 1 CORINTHIANS 4:2

We care for anything for which we work, and especially for which we sacrifice a little, you know.

"Who for the joy that was set before him endured the cross, despising the shame, and is set down at the right hand of the throne of God." HEBREWS 12:2

I tremble for any man whose will is not anchored on the rock Christ Jesus.

"Which hope we have as an anchor of the soul, both sure and steadfast, and which entereth into that within the veil." HEBREWS 6:19

Shall we who belong to Christ's body have aught to say against the different members of that body? Don't you think it is a subject that we, as Christians, need to think much of? Do we not constantly forget that we are "members one of another"?

"Now ye are the body of Christ, and members in particular."
1 CORINTHIANS 12:27

"I am *not* a prisoner," she told herself firmly, "nor a slave. I am the Lord's free woman. I am responsible to Him; and I will not bow my neck to the yoke of fashionable life. I will not appear to countenance what I do not approve."

"Stand fast, therefore, in the liberty wherewith Christ hath made us free, and be not entangled with the yoke of bondage." GALATIANS 5:2

Suppose we actually bore on our hearts the individual griefs of the world? How long would our poor bodies be in breaking under the strain?

"Surely he hath borne our griefs, and carried our sorrows."
ISAIAH 53:4

Poor, tired heart. Don't you think that the Lord Jesus can rest you anywhere except by the way of the grave? Don't you hear His voice calling to you to come and rest in Him this minute?

"Come unto me, all ye that labor and are heavy laden, and I will give you rest."   MATTHEW 11:28

SEPTEMBER 20TH

It was the humiliation of this Christian woman that there were times when silence would have been golden, in which she could not resist the temptation to sarcasm.

"To everything there is a season, and a time to every purpose under the heaven. . . .
A time to keep silence, and a time to speak."   ECCLESIASTES 3:7

SEPTEMBER 21ST

There is so much religion in these days that wants to be done up in pink cotton and laid safely away from human sight and sound.

"I pray not that thou shouldst take them out of the world, but that thou shouldst keep them from the evil one."   JOHN 17:15

SEPTEMBER 22ND

She had been so long among people who did not know how to pray, as to have almost forgotten how busy some women were in their Lord's vineyard.

"Even so, then, at this present time also, there is a remnant according to the election of grace."   ROMANS 11:5

SEPTEMBER 23RD

He considered himself posted on all subjects, whether in art, literature, or music; and unhesitatingly expressed his opinion with an air that was intended to quench any opposing views from any source whatever. I do not think he would have hesitated to dispute the most eminent scientist which the world has produced, if he happened to venture a statement not in accordance with his own preconceived opinion, though that opinion might have been adopted because of a chance remark which he heard some one make at the breakfast table."

"Seest thou a man wise in his own conceit? there is more hope of a fool than of him." PROVERBS 26:12

SEPTEMBER 24TH

It is easier to be good for others than it is for one's self.

"Therefore thou art inexcusable, O man, whosoever thou art that judgest: for wherein thou judgest another, thou condemnest thyself; for thou that judgest doest the same things." ROMANS 2:1

SEPTEMBER 25TH

She had not wanted to wrap herself in black for her father. It was true that she felt desolate enough to describe it to the world by the heaviest crêpe it could furnish her; but, remembering her father's face, as earth receded from him, and Heaven appeared, remembering the smile of unearthly radiance with which he finally "entered in," it had not seemed fitting that she, a Christian, looking forward to the same entrance one day, should array herself in gloom, and mourn as those who had no bright side to their sorrow.

"I will turn their mourning into joy, and I will comfort them, and make them rejoice from their sorrow." JEREMIAH 31:13

We love to be governed by reason, and hate to walk in the dark. I have always wondered what Philip said when called to leave his great meeting, where it seemed hardly possible to do without him, and go toward the south on a desert road. That he went, and promptly, is, I think, a wonderful thing for Philip.

"For now we see through a glass, darkly; but then face to face: now I know in part; but then shall I know even as also I am known."
1 CORINTHIANS 13:12

"Whosoever shall do the will of my Father which is in Heaven, the same is my brother and sister." If they are *His* brothers and sisters then are they not ours, if we belong to His family? and you know we do not like to see our kindred subjects of ridicule, even though they may sometimes be guilty of bad taste in dress, and have among them those who have physical infirmities.

"For he that toucheth you toucheth the apple of his eye."
ZECHARIAH 2:8

Union with Christ; such a union as carries you captive — making your time, and your money, and your talents, not your own, but His. There is nothing dissatisfying about such a life, my friend. It almost lifts one above the accident of outward surroundings.

"But none of these things move me, neither count I my life dear unto myself, so that I might finish my course with joy." ACTS 20:24

It seemed to Ruth, afterwards, that during that half-hour after the doctor left her alone, she came face to face with a realizing sense of death and the judgment, for the first time in her life! And the thought that a soul with which she had had to do, for years, was going swiftly forward into those scenes, all unprepared, seemed almost to paralyze her with terror.

"They watch for your souls, as they that must give account, that they may do it with joy, and not with grief."   HEBREWS 13:17

It is a blessed thing that the just God is more tender and pitiful than men and women.

"I will heal their backsliding, I will love them freely: for mine anger is turned away from him."   HOSEA 14:4

OCTOBER

"Go tell my disciples — and Peter." Just think of that! A special message to Peter, the one who had treated him the worst.

> *"Oh! see how Jesus trusts himself*
> *Unto our childish love,*
> *As though by his free ways with us,*
> *Our earnestness to prove."*

"Times are changed, and I like the Lord's house to keep pace with our own, at least. Look how they did with the Temple. The Lord had the best used for that. It came first, and I suppose if the people had anything left, they could put some of the pretty into their own homes, but not before the Temple had all it needed. That ought to be the rule now," said Mrs. Smith.

"And they spake unto Moses, saying, The people bring much more than enough for the service of the work." EXODUS 36:5

Two souls ought to be able to come together in communion with the Master every evening. There is a good deal of wasted happiness in this world.

"Again I say unto you, That if two of you shall agree on earth as touching anything that they shall ask, it shall be done for them of my Father which is in heaven." MATTHEW 18:19

"If I have resolved to strive to do whatever He would like to have me, there can be no objection to my writing the resolution on paper for the purpose of letting others know where I stand, and of winning them to my way. Of course the signing a covenant is merely the expression for the convenience of others, of a deliberate conviction and line of action. Whether I set down my name, or not, does not alter the facts as they stand revealed to the Lord Jesus Christ."

"I believed, therefore have I spoken; I will walk before the Lord in the land of the living. I will pay my vows unto the Lord." PSALM 116:10

It is a strange thing, and a solemn thing to realize how unwittingly the seed of unbelief may be sown in a young heart.

"Take heed what ye do." 2 CHRONICLES 19:6

Alas! for the doctors who shrink away from death as a grim monster, and know nothing about the Hand of Power that has taken away the sting. No wonder that the temptation to shirk or to deliberately deny the truth is too great for them.

"O, death! where is thy sting? O, grave! where is thy victory?"

1 CORINTHIANS 15:55

OCTOBER 7TH

Human patience is a very weak and contemptible thing, but if you belong to the Lord Jesus Christ, you have found in Him infinite patience, and it is His command that you struggle to make this patience yours; to watch over, and weep for, and pray for the fallen with Christ-like patience and Christ-like tenacity.

"But let patience have her perfect work, that ye may be perfect and entire, wanting nothing."

JAMES 1:4

OCTOBER 8TH

When we stop and consider it, life, for the most part, is made up of little things. It is only the occasional which is startling in its magnitude.

"Who knoweth not in all these that the hand of the Lord hath wrought this?
In whose hand is the soul of every living thing."

JOB 12:9

OCTOBER 9TH

It is not every one who, having made arrangements to give a party, goes to his Father in Heaven for help and encouragement.

"And the third day there was a marriage in Cana of Galilee; and the mother of Jesus was there:
And both Jesus was called, and his disciples, to the marriage."   JOHN 2:1

He discoursed learnedly on religious topics, making the wildest statements, which were without even the shadow of a solid foundation, and proceeding gravely to argue about them as the accepted standards of the Church.

"Who is this that darkeneth counsel by words without knowledge?"
    JOB 38:2

Do you suppose St. Paul had to patronize fairs, and buy slippers and things, for the benefit of churches in Ephesus or Corinth?

"And all that believed were together, and had all things common;
And sold their possessions and goods, and parted them to all men, as every man had need."   ACTS 2:44

No heavy burdens, so-called, but ten thousand little things, or what in our parlance are called little things, weighed down her heart, fettered her lips, and filled her with a steadily increasing unrest.

"And Jesus answered and said unto her, Martha, Martha, thou art careful and troubled about many things."   LUKE 10:41

What are homes for? Why did He give you one? May it not possibly be that He wants you to show its photograph to others for a purpose?

"My lord, O king, according to thy saying, I am thine, and all that I have." 1 KINGS 20:4

I think if I could help to lead one person to understand and love the Lord Jesus Christ as much even as I understand Him now, so that He would be that soul's eternal salvation, it would be ambition enough to fill a lifetime.

"O, Jerusalem, Jerusalem, thou that killest the prophets, and stonest them which are sent unto thee, how often would I have gathered thy children together, even as a hen gathereth her chickens under her wings, and ye would not!" MATTHEW 23:37

Perhaps it is just as well for young people to look squarely in the face the fact that there will be discouragements to meet their hopes, and apathetic croakers to meet their enthusiasms, to the end of time.

The main thing, and the central pivot on which the main thing will turn, is to make sure of being able to say bravely to your inmost soul: "The Lord is with us, fear them not."

"The slothful man saith, 'there is a lion in the way.'" PROVERBS 26:13
"And there we saw the giants! And we were in our own sight as grasshoppers." NUMBERS 13:33

She felt that the time had certainly come when she could no longer fold her hands in graceful idleness; she must find her appointed niche in the Lord's great workshop, and do her part.

"And straightway he (Paul) preached Christ in the synagogues."
ACTS 9:20

Jeanie Barret, when she knelt in that tented space, felt only a blind, homesick longing for an experience such as she believed some had, but which she was more than doubtful could be for her. When she arose, not ten minutes afterward, she knew, as well as that she stood there, with the old minister touching her arm and speaking to her in low tones, that she had passed from the position which she had all her life occupied over to the other side, with the Lord Jesus Christ for her advocate.

"One thing I know, that, whereas I was blind, now I see."   JOHN 9:25

There are mornings trying to the souls of cooks, when it is well known that the kettle will not boil until it is waited for, and coaxed with special chips, and then it chooses an unexpected moment and boils over into the potatoes, and steak smokes instead of broils, and everything everywhere is totally depraved.

"And lest I should be exalted above measure through the abundance of the revelations, there was given to me a thorn in the flesh, the messenger of Satan to buffet me, lest I should be exalted above measure."   2 CORINTHIANS 12:7

As for herself, she had full and abiding faith in the fact that the Christ of Galilee had lavished miracles, many and wonderful, upon that favored people eighteen hundred years ago; what she wanted was a miracle for her, to-day.

"But Naaman was wroth, and went away, and said, Behold, I thought, he will surely come out to me, and stand, and call on the name of the Lord his God, and strike his hand over the place, and recover the leper."　　　　　　　　　　　　　　　　　2 KINGS 5:11

I wonder if everything about us, rightly managed, would become a talent?

"And the Lord said unto him, What is that in thine hand? And he said, A rod."　　　　　　　　　　　　　　　　　EXODUS 4:2

What wonderful rewards God may have in store for even our smallest efforts made for His sake!

"The Lord recompense thy work, and a full reward be given thee of the Lord God of Israel, under whose wings thou art come to trust."　　　　RUTH 2:12

There is no class of workers more utterly to be pitied than those who struggle and toil, "making bricks" oftentimes "without straw," and who find at the close that, someway, the bricks seem not to have been worth the cost.

"Wherefore do ye spend money for that which is not bread? and your labor for that which satisfieth not? hearken diligently unto me, and eat ye that which is good, and let your soul delight itself in fatness."　　　　ISAIAH 55:2

OCTOBER 23RD

Don't you know that people are in strips? Whenever I see a new face I can calculate in a few minutes from which strip it came.

"And being let go, they went to their own company."　　　　ACTS 4:23

OCTOBER 24TH

Talk about woman's intuition! Let me assure you that there are some women, or it may be they are only girls, before time and bitter experience have taught them the hard wisdom of the world, whose faith in those whom they love is so absolute that nothing has power to shake it.

"Love covereth all sins."　　　　PROVERBS 10:12

OCTOBER 25TH

You cannot have lived in this world so long without discovering that pain and disappointment of every sort are not happenings, but have their own wise and most important ends to fulfill, though we may be too childish to see the occasion, or understand the remedy.

"Thou shalt also consider in thine heart, that, as a man chasteneth his son, so the Lord thy God chasteneth thee."　　　　DEUTERONOMY 8:5

I wonder to what extent the gracious Spirit of God hovers near to suggest and help those who never ask for His help?

"That they should seek the Lord, if haply they might feel after Him, and find Him, though He be not far from every one of us."   ACTS 17:27

You and I and most of the Christian world are trying to make ourselves good. We are willing to trust Christ for salvation from punishment, but as for trusting Him to keep our feet from falling, we don't mean to do any such thing. We are going to look after our own feet, and teach them by gradual steps, by the law of progression, the law of growth, and any other law that we can bring to bear on it, to attain to a state of goodness, not to be kept to-day, but to attain next year to a place where we can keep ourselves. Isn't that it?

"Who are kept by the power of God through faith unto salvation ready to be revealed in the last time."   1 PETER 1:5

It was a surprising thing when one stopped to look at it; she, a Christian woman, hurrying to an emergency which she consciously did not know how to meet, yet taking no time to consult the acknowledged Source of all wisdom, not only, but One who had graciously said, "Ask of me."

"And ye shall be brought before governors and kings for my sake, for a testimony against them and the Gentiles.
But when they deliver you up, take no thought how or what ye shall speak: for it shall be given you in that same hour what ye shall speak."
MATTHEW 10:18, 19

Don't you know there are things, legions of things, that you cannot explain to some people? You may lay bare your heart, though it quiver over the intrusion, and they will step on it, and ask: "Why is this?" and "Of what use is that?" and "What does the other mean?" until, unless you are a saint, you flee from them in dismay.

"For thou hast hid their heart from understanding." JOB 17:4

"She had just been brought face to face with a new and solemn joy, which is unlike any other joy to be experienced this side of Heaven; and which can no more be described than one can describe the air we breathe, or the Heaven to which we are going. She had been permitted of the Lord, to speak such words as had moved the soul of a young man — a young man who was in peril. He had been more than moved emotionally; that tremendous potentate — the human will — had spoken. "I will do it," the young man had said, and she knew that a decision for eternity had been made.

"For this cause also thank we God without ceasing, because when ye received the word of God which ye heard of us, ye received it not as the word of men, but as it is in truth, the word of God." 1 THESSALONIANS 2:13

I have been wondering how many of us are children of the same family traveling towards home, and failing to recognize the kinship on the way.

"And they shall see his face; and his name shall be in their foreheads."
REVELATION 22:4

NOVEMBER

"I am that young man to whom you, on that never-to-be-forgotten Sunday, made plain as daylight the way to eternal life. I thought you ought to know that I kept my promise to go straight to the Lord Jesus and claim His help. And I got it, bless His name! I belong to Him now, in life and death."

Was ever sweeter music than this offered to a Christian's ears?

"They that be wise shall shine as the brightness of the firmament; and they that turn many to righteousness as the stars forever and ever."
DANIEL 12:3

"Every spot in this house is historic ground," Ermina declared one morning, after a closely-contested argument had been held. "Helen and Maria have a battle in every room and on every chair."

"Him that is weak in the faith receive ye, but not to doubtful disputations."
ROMANS 14:1

"Of course she had her own peculiar views as to what happiness really was, and to say that she sometimes came to grief by the very road which she supposed led to Paradise, is to admit no more than falls to the lot of mortals older and wiser than herself."

"Ask counsel, we pray thee, of God, that we may know whether our very way which we go shall be prosperous." JUDGES 18:5

NOVEMBER 4TH

"Just think! What if His memory were no better than our poor weak ones! We cannot remember even the names of our friends!"

"What is man, that thou art mindful of him? and the son of man, that thou visitest him?" PSALM 8:4

NOVEMBER 5TH

I never like to fight Satan with his own weapons, he understands everything pertaining to his business so much better than we do.

"Wherefore, take unto you the whole armor of God, that ye may be able to withstand in the evil day, and having done all, to stand." EPHESIANS 6:13

NOVEMBER 6TH

I have unquestioning faith in the truth that even our mistakes He will overrule for our good.

"And we know that all things work together for good to them that love God, to them who are the called according to his purpose." ROMANS 8:28

We are willing to be cleansed in the Jordan, but after that, we want to see to it ourselves that we do not get sick again, and because we fail, because we find that we cannot attain to perfect health, any more than we could cure ourselves of leprosy, instead of resting in the strength of One who has said His grace was sufficient, and that He was able to keep us from falling, we go right on sinning and repenting and assuring ourselves that such is the way, and that with such living the Lord who redeemed us must be content. He mustn't expect us to trust Him entirely, until we get away from earth. Is that fair?

"Being confident of this very thing, that he which hath begun a good work in you will perform it until the day of Jesus Christ."
PHILIPPIANS 1:6

Did God design that through the channel of song she should be led up to Him?

What a grand thing it would be to have that voice sing only His praise!

"And, lo, thou art unto them as a very lovely song of one that hath a pleasant voice, and can play well on an instrument."   EZEKIEL 33:32

"In God's great field of labor
All work is not the same;
He hath a service for each one
Who loves His holy name.
And you to whom the secrets
Of all sweet sounds are known,
Rise up! for He hath called you
To a mission of your own."

People will not be warned; they will just go and throw everything away, just as Absalom did. I suppose he did it all for the sake of ambition. I don't know whether, after all, that don't indicate a trifle more character than to do it for fun. That is what people seem to be after nowadays.

"He that pursueth evil pursueth it to his own death."   PROVERBS 11:19

"What difference do you suppose it makes to me what people think? 'To his own master he standeth or falleth.' That is Scripture, I believe," declared the aristocratic aunt.

"That's true," said Mrs. Smith, in no wise quenched. "That's true enough so far as the judging of other folks is concerned; the Lord wants to do that Himself, because He understands all the little hidden things that we know nothing about; but I guess it don't apply to folks not caring what other people think of 'em, because the Lord told us to be careful about that."

"Moreover, he must have a good report of them which are without; lest he fall into reproach and the snare of the devil."   1 TIMOTHY 3:7

The building is the outward sign of His presence, is it not? And suggests one of the ways in which we can show our love for the God to whose worship the Church is dedicated.

"If I forget thee, O, Jerusalem! let my right hand forget her cunning."
PSALM 137:5

"If you do not try to understand the people who are of another world than yours — to, in short, 'put yourselves in their places,' occasionally — how do you expect to be other than narrow and cold in your charities?"

"Finally, be ye all of one mind, having compassion one of another, love as brethren."   1 PETER 3:8

Suppose I were Paul, and should come to call on you this evening, and should say to you, "Have you received the Holy Ghost since you believed?" what would you answer?

"And I will pray the Father, and he shall give you another Comforter, that he may abide with you forever."   JOHN 14:16

The clear, cultured voice went on; "Young man, God is speaking to you; He wants you; wants you to-day; wants your brains, and your strength, and your influence, for Himself. Why do you wait? You know you need Him."

"He calleth thee."   MARK 10:49

A very little child can learn to love the Saviour.

"Samuel ministered before the Lord, being a child."   1 SAMUEL 2:18

It is better to give over planning the side that your arm is too weak to reach, and learn to trust.

"What is that to thee? follow thou me." JOHN 21:22

Only think of it, whiter than snow! That is our privilege, to stand before God so white that even the whitest thing we know is shadowed, in comparison; and yet how little we try for it; how little of the whiteness we are willing to accept. We seem rather anxious to have the soiled garments left about us.

"Come now, and let us reason together, saith the Lord: though your sins be as scarlet, they shall be as white as snow; though they be red like crimson, they shall be as wool." ISAIAH 1:18

But do you think it is wise to spend your time in studying the imperfect copies, without looking at the perfect pattern? You would not take the child's careless imitation as a proof that his teacher could not write.

"I am the Almighty God; walk before me, and be thou perfect."
GENESIS 17:1

I never realized, until a few days ago, that I was trusting myself instead of Christ. I have even felt a sort of complacency at night when thinking over the day. "I have done wrong in that thing," I said, "and in that, but in that other matter I came off conqueror. I am stronger to-day than I was last week. Oh! well, that is encouraging; I can't, of course, expect to be perfect all in a minute. I can only keep pressing on." Now, whose goodness is that but mine? Whom am I trusting? Who do I mean cannot make me free from my besetting sins in a minute?

"Without me ye can do nothing." JOHN 15:5

NOVEMBER 20TH

Who can tell what God may let those little hands or that baby voice do for His glory in the turning of the nations?

"Out of the mouth of babes and sucklings thou hast perfected praise."
MATTHEW 21:16

NOVEMBER 21ST

Who will undertake to describe a *soul?*

"Who knoweth the spirit of man that goeth upward."
ECCLESIASTES 3:21

NOVEMBER 22ND

"She had come to a place where two roads met, and one was a narrow and possibly somewhat stony pathway, but ever leading upward, and growing broader and brighter as it neared the heights of the entrance gate to the Eternal City; while the other was a distinct downward plunge."

"There is a line by us unseen,
That crosses every path;
That marks the boundary between
God's mercy and His wrath."

"There is a way which seemeth right unto a man, but the end thereof
are the ways of death."   PROVERBS 14:12

"The expulsive power of a new affection."
I often think of that sentence in one of my old text books. It works magic with the human heart.

"If any man love me, he will keep my words: and my Father will love him,
and we will come unto him, and make our abode with him."   JOHN 14:23

Suppose every lecturer were called upon to explain the meaning of the words he used! What would become of the lecturer?

"Who is he that hideth counsel without knowledge? therefore have I uttered
that I understand not; things too wonderful for me, which I knew not."
JOB 42:3

You cannot see the heart. Only the Lord can see that, and it is only the Lord who has, therefore, a right to judge.

"But Jesus did not commit himself unto them, because he knew all men,
And needed not that any should testify of man: for he knew what was in
man."   JOHN 2:24

All the combined wisdom of the world, though it was poured into
my ears in the form of arguments to which I could make no answer in
words, could not convince me that God does not hear my prayer and
answer: because I have daily proof from Himself that He does just
that thing.

"In my distress I called upon the Lord, and cried to my God: and He did
hear my voice out of His temple, and my cry did enter into His ears."
                                                                    2 SAMUEL 22:7

Isn't it cowardly to mind a laugh, when the road we want to take is
not only the most sensible, but the only safe one to take?

"Blessed are ye that weep now: for ye shall laugh."   LUKE 6:21

"But one must stand somewhere. Either you are willing to try to
please the Lord Jesus Christ *to-day*, or else you are not willing. There is
no middle ground."

"Choose ye this day whom ye will serve."   JOSHUA 24:15
"If the Lord be God, follow him."   1 KINGS 18:21

"It would be curious to trace the laws of influence, and see in what remote quarters they touch; and how strangely unlike the starting-point is the message which is brought to some."

"That which is far off, and exceeding deep, who can find it out?"
ECCLESIASTES 7:24
"But He knoweth the way that I take." JOB 23:10

Ah, well, they lived through it. It is surprising how many trials we do succeed in pushing through, and coming out alive on the other side!

"These are they which came out of great tribulation, and have washed their robes, and made them white in the blood of the Lamb."
REVELATION 7:14

DECEMBER

A year is only a half-hour in Heaven.

"But, beloved, be not ignorant of this one thing, that one day is with the Lord as a thousand years, and a thousand years as one day."   2 PETER 3:8

> *"When we've been there ten thousand years,*
> *Bright shining as the sun,*
> *We've no less days to sing God's praise,*
> *than when we first begun."*

I doubt if there are any chains harder to break than sleepy ones.

"Therefore, let us not sleep, as do others; but let us watch and be sober."
1 THESSALONIANS 5:6

God meant that the human will should be a great engine for good, but the human will perverted, is a rotten plank, on which one's weight cannot be trusted.

"I seek not mine own will, but the will of the Father which hath sent me."   JOHN 5:30

"And says Solomon, 'I s'pose if we had *growin'* faith like a grain of mustard seed — that doesn't stay a grain, after it is planted, but grows up into a tree — if we was like that, we would keep amazing folks all the time; they would say they never saw the like! And they would *have* to glorify God whether they wanted to or not. The trouble is, we ain't mustard trees at all, but poor little dwarf plants; we don't die outright, and that's about all that can be said of us.' "

"And immediately he arose, took up the bed, and went forth before them all; insomuch that they were all amazed, and glorified God, saying, We never saw it on this fashion."   MARK 2:12

I will give you a general rule, which I have found a great benefit in my Christian life. If you find there is the least doubt in your mind as to the right or wrong of a certain path, give Christ the benefit of the doubt and you will surely be right.

"And he that doubteth is condemned."   ROMANS 14:23

If all honest unbelievers would but stop their reasoning, trying to plan out God's work for Him, and go to Him with the whole story, how quickly it would silence all doubt. For faith is the gift of God.

"If any man will do His will, he shall know of the doctrine, whether it be of God, or whether I speak of myself."　　　　JOHN 7:17

DECEMBER 7TH

Some sorrowful places there may be for your feet and mine on our journey home. Bear the thorns of the way in patience, for they are only *on the way* through the woods; not a thorn in the home.

"For I reckon that the sufferings of this present time are not worthy to be compared with the glory which shall be revealed in us."　　　　ROMANS 8:18

DECEMBER 8TH

Remember that no early mistake can be righted by adding to it a later and a graver one.

"And the king was sorry: nevertheless, for the oath's sake, and them which sat with him at meat, he commanded it to be given her."　　　　MATTHEW 14:9

DECEMBER 9TH

If you could be sure that the hand of the Lord was really in every phase of life, how greatly would it tone and temper all the experiences thereof!

"Behold the fowls of the air: for they sow not, neither do they reap, nor gather into barns; yet your Heavenly Father feedeth them. Are ye not much better than they?"　　　　MATTHEW 6:26

"In the meantime, what you and I find in the Bible that God has spoken, we will try to do, always: whether it is hard or easy. Shall we not?"

"If ye keep my commandments, ye shall abide in my love; even as I have kept my Father's commandments, and abide in his love."   JOHN 15:10

"There is no respect of persons with God."
What is the use in a man thinking about his "position" or his "abilities" after that?

"My brethren, have not the faith of our Lord Jesus Christ, the Lord of glory, with respect of persons."   JAMES 2:1

"It is not heavy trials always which unnerve us. Our Christian faith often rises superior to these, when a pin-prick would move us to tears."

"Though now for a season, if need be, ye are in heaviness through manifold temptations:
That the trial of your faith being more precious than that of gold that perisheth, though it be tried with fire, might be found unto praise and honor and glory at the appearing of Jesus Christ."   1 PETER 1:6-7

I know, I have to be careful of making conditions, when it comes to a matter of prayer. It is the Lord's right to make conditions if He will; but it is not mine.

"And this is the confidence that we have in him, that, if we ask any-thing according to his will, he heareth us." 1 JOHN 5:14

I should like to know if even a *little* knowledge isn't better than ignorance! Suppose a stream isn't very deep; if it is water that we need, it is much better than no stream at all, isn't it?

"And she said, Truth, Lord: yet the dogs eat of the crumbs which fall from their masters' table." MATTHEW 15:27

Certain sopranos were asked to prepare choice selections, such as: "I think only of thee, Love," and "My Heart's dearest Treasure," and "Ever thine own, Love," and a few other of those gems which we hear screamed out by seraphic voices to large and appreciative audiences. I have never heard it explained why so much of our popular music should be wedded to words which the performer would blush to repeat in prose to an audience of more than one.

"It is better to hear the rebuke of the wise, than for a man to hear the song of fools." ECCLESIASTES 7:15

The Lord will have nothing to do with compromises. When He has made the right entirely plain to you, the manner in which you may be sustained, while you are treading the road of His pointing out, is in a sense not your concern; He will undertake for you. Trust Him.

"Hath the Lord as great delight in burnt offerings and sacrifices, as in obeying the voice of the Lord? Behold, to obey is better than sacrifice."

1 SAMUEL 15:22

It is noticeable that when we get down to the root of the matter and question how the Lord Himself views us, instead of what human eyes see and human hearts think, we forget the mote in our brother's eye and busy ourselves solemnly with the beam in our own eye.

"Behold, I am vile; what shall I answer thee? I will lay mine hand upon my mouth."

JOB 40:4

Sometimes I have heard people talk as though they really thought there was a different code of rules for a minister's life, than for the ordinary Christian's. But, after all, he has to be guided by the same Bible, led by the same Spirit.

"And, let every one that nameth the name of Christ depart from iniquity."

2 PETER 2:19

It often happens that what we cannot find in this world ready made to our needs, we proceed to manufacture.

"And when they could not come nigh unto him for the press, they uncovered the roof where he was: and when they had broken it up, they let down the bed wherein the sick of the palsy lay."

MARK 2:4

I was as certainly chosen of God as ever Paul was; for assuredly I did not come to Him of myself, and therefore He must indeed have chosen me; and I wonder whether probably each Christian has not a work to do as definite as Paul's — a work that would be given to no other, unless indeed the chosen one failed.

"The God of our fathers hath chosen thee, that thou shouldest know his will."   ACTS 22:14

The Lord met Saul and gave him wonderful salvation, but He didn't save him from many a future trial and pain. He never promised to do so.

"For whom the Lord loveth he chasteneth, and scourgeth every son whom he receiveth."   HEBREWS 12:6

Who lives exclamation points every day? There comes occasionally one, into most lives; but, for the most part, lives are made up of commas, and interrogations, and dashes.

"My times are in thy hand."   PSALM 31:15

"He was not the sort of man who could frankly say, 'I was in the wrong, I beg you will forgive.' Such a statement calls for a very high grade of character; calls, perhaps for Christian character; though there have been men who knew how to say 'forgive me,' to mortals, not yet having learned to say it to Christ!"

"Humble yourselves in the sight of the Lord, and he shall lift you up."
JAMES 4:10

DECEMBER 24TH

I don't know the end of any story that is being lived now — yours or mine, for instance; but the Lord does; and I would much rather have Him do all the planning.

"But he knoweth the way that I take: when he hath tried me, I shall come forth as gold."
JOB 23:10

"His wisdom ever waketh,
His sight is never dim;
He knows the way He taketh,
And I will walk with Him."

DECEMBER 25TH

"Said I to Jessie: 'That's for all the world the way your Uncle Solomon acts when he gets in the house a little before dinner is ready. He looks at the clock, and he watches me, and he gapes, and he acts as though there was nothing in the world he was so near ready for as his dinner, till I get it on the table, and say, "Come, Solomon," and then he's off. He finds out that the gate isn't shut, and that the stove in the front room needs a stick of wood, and his hands need washing, and there's no end to the things that he seems to think he must do while the dinner sets there and spoils.' "

"In all things shewing thyself a pattern of good works."   TITUS 2:7

You know reasons can almost always be found for things, when we are very anxious to find them.

"In which are some things hard to be understood, which they that are unlearned and unstable wrest, as they do also the other scriptures, unto their own destruction."
2 PETER 3:16

At last Miranda's whispered cries in his ear, and her gentle shakings aroused the boy to a sense of his surroundings. . . . For an instant a wild thought of his own mother whom he had never known came to him and then almost immediately he knew that it was Miranda. All the hideous truth of his situation came back to him, as life tragedies will on sudden waking, yet the strong young arms, that with their efforts were warm, and the soft breath and exquisitely soft cheek were there.

"And lo, I am with you alway, even unto the end of the world."
MATTHEW 28:20

Why do we, any of us, allow temper, and neuralgia, and colds in the head, to get the better of us? I'm sure I don't know; but haven't you done it?

"And he said unto me, My grace is sufficient for thee: for my strength is made perfect in weakness. Most gladly therefore will I glory in my infirmities, that the power of Christ may rest upon me."
2 CORINTHIANS 12:9

Suppose we knew all the histories of all the happenings of one day? With what awe, and dismay, and terror, and gratitude, they might fill us, according as we had, with our little thoughtless words and ways, helped or hindered the march of a soul!

"Be not deceived; God is not mocked; for whatsoever a man soweth, that shall he also reap."　　　　　　　　　　　GALATIANS 6:7

"Some day, mother, he will slip away from the hedges with which your love has surrounded him.

"You have not fed him with reasons for things. So many mothers are failing here."

"Train up a child in the way he should go: and when he is old, he will not depart from it."　　　　　　　　　PROVERBS 22:16

Acts that involve a lifetime of trouble can be told in a few words.

"It is finished."　　　　　　　　　　　　　　JOHN 19:30